MAYA

MAYA

THE BIOGRAPHY OF A TIGER

ANANT SONAWANE

HarperCollins *Publishers* India

First published in English in India by HarperCollins *Publishers* 2026
Building 10-A, Gurugram, Haryana – 122002, India
www.harpercollins.co.in

2 4 6 8 10 9 7 5 3 1

Originally published in Marathi as *Ek Hoti Maya* by Tadoba–Andhari Tiger Reserve Conservation Foundation, Chandrapur, 2024

P-ISBN: 978-93-6569-441-3
E-ISBN: 978-93-6569-805-3

Printed and bound at Magic International Pvt. Ltd., India

*

HarperCollins Publishers, Macken House, 39/40 Mayor Street Upper, Dublin 1, D01 C9W8, Ireland

FOR MAYA,
the heartbeat of millions
and every soul who loved her
with a devotion
as wild as the forests she ruled

Foreword

Some places stay with you long after you leave them. The Tadoba-Andhari Tiger reserve is one of those places for me. Over the years my family and I have returned to its forests again and again, not to escape life but to feel closer to something real and grounding. We've visited tiger reserves across the country and national parks in other parts of the world, but Tadoba has a one-of-a-kind temperament. It makes you slow down. It makes you pay attention.

If you spend enough time here, the forest starts to feel familiar. The tigers do, too. They stop being just quick sightings and begin to feel like individuals. You hear stories about them. You learn who is related to whom, who commands which part of the forest. Names start to carry weight. In Tadoba, those names are remembered by everyone, whether it be guides and forest staff or drivers, photographers and tourists who come back year after year. Maya was one such name. You heard it often, uttered with respect and admiration.

Maya's renown did not come from mere spectacle. It came from the way in which she held her ground while living in a forest under constant human watch—from her calm, her confidence and the certainty of her movements. Despite the many stories about her posing for cameras, she was never tame or predictable. She moved through this shared space at her own pace—alert but undisturbed. That kind of presence is rare.

Maya had the charisma that you never hear of in tigers. She enchanted people and left them mesmerized, whetting their appetite for more of her. No wonder Maya became the most sought-after tigress in the wild by the humans, and arguably the most photographed wild tiger in the world.

In October 2023, when news of her disappearance came in, it

was deeply unsettling for many of us who care about this forest. There was worry, but also a quieter discomfort. We know that life in the wild offers no certainty and no clear answers, but that knowledge does not make loss easier to accept.

What Anant Sonawane does in this book is resist the pull of that final moment. Instead, he takes us back to the life Maya lived. He follows her story from her early vulnerability to the time she became a strong and dominant tiger in the forest. His writing is careful and clear, allowing Maya to remain what she always was—a wild animal on her own terms.

Reading this book brought back many hours I have spent in Tadoba—waiting, watching, learning to notice small changes in the daily lives of these animals. It reminded me why stories like this matter. They make us curious about wildlife and sharpen our understanding of these creatures, while also reminding us that the animals we admire are living beings trying to survive in landscapes shaped by human presence.

Tadoba has given me moments of awe and perspective over the years. Maya's life is part of that experience. This book honours it with restraint and care.

SACHIN TENDULKAR
5 January 2026

Did You See Her?

1 October 2023: The Moharli Gate buzzed with excitement. As the primary entryway into the core forest zone of Tadoba–Andhari, Maharashtra, it is always a busy site during the morning and afternoon safari hours. But on this particular morning, there was something extraordinary in the air redolent of a festive ritual.

The iron entry gate was adorned with marigold garlands. Neatly arranged beside it were boxes of sweets, garlands, coconuts and other ceremonial items. There was no band, no loudspeakers blaring songs, yet the charged energy in the air made plenty of noise on its own. The local sarpanch, village residents, forest officials, safari guides, Gypsy drivers, resort owners, tourists and reporters had all gathered. Excitement radiated from every gesture, every conversation.

The 2023 tourism season began without any sighting of her

What was so special about this day?

As mandated by the National Tiger Conservation Authority (NTCA), tourism in the reserve's core zone is suspended from 1 July to 30 September, during the monsoon month, to prevent tourist vehicles from getting stuck on the rain-soaked mud roads. Tourism continues only in the buffer zones—home to human settlements and activities. The core forest, however, remains undisturbed, with only forest department personnel permitted entry. Even during the tourism season, tourists are allowed in just 20 per cent of the area during designated hours. 1 October heralds the reopening of the season, and the first safari understandably becomes a celebration.

Visitors had arrived from across India—and overseas—to witness this annual spectacle. At exactly 5.30 a.m., a pristine white Scorpio arrived carrying Field Director Dr Jitendra Ramgaokar. Accompanied by the Sarpanch, he performed a pooja, broke a coconut and officially inaugurated the tourism season. Sweets were handed out as TV reporters jostled for interviews with the field director.

At the gate, the staff began checking safari tickets and verifying IDs. Tourists exchanged cheerful wishes: 'Have a great sighting!' and 'All the best!' One by one, the jeeps rolled in through the gate and into the jungle.

By around 10 a.m., the jeeps started to return. A single question echoed among the visitors: 'Did you see her?'

The answers were disappointing. Some had spotted Balram or Bajrang, while others had caught a glimpse of Sonam, Lara or Roma. But no one had seen her.

The afternoon safari ended with the same result—no sightings of her! The second day came and went. Then the third, fourth and fifth—each day adding to the growing worry among her fans.

Finally, on 6 October, *The Times of India* ran a headline capturing the growing mystery: 'Where Has Tadoba's Queen Maya Gone?'

A Dark Day

It was 7 a.m., and October was nearing its end. A cool winter nip was beginning to set in. The entire forest basked in the soft golden sunlight. Spotted deer grazed cautiously by Tadoba Lake, while a crocodile lay sunbathing nearby. Cormorants and ducks stirred the waters occasionally. On this quiet morning, Nibuddhe, a field assistant at Khatoda and his team, set out on patrol.

Foot patrols are a crucial aspect of forest department's work. Each guard is required to cover at least 125 kilometres on foot every month. The patrol teams, comprising three to five members, traverse vast areas of the jungle, primarily to prevent poaching, illegal logging and grazing. It's dangerous work—they can unexpectedly encounter tigers, leopards, sloth bears, Indian gaurs, snakes or scorpions. Vigilance is paramount.

Nibuddhe and his team moved cautiously. Their trained eyes and ears stayed alert to even the subtlest movement. After circling the lake, they reached the main road. Just then, a tourist Gypsy approached from Pandharpauni. As it neared, the driver brought the vehicle to a halt. Typically, safari guides pause briefly to enquire if the forest staff has noticed any movement of tigers. But today, this Gypsy had stopped for a different reason.

The tourists inside appeared anxious, and the guide and driver were visibly tense.

'Sir, I'm Tulshi Ramteke,' said the guide.

'What happened?' Nibuddhe asked.

'Sir ... there's a tiger.'

'What about it?' Nibuddhe's voice rose instinctively.

'It's lying dead!'

'What? Where?'

'On the Jamni checkpost—Waghai road, in the nallah (seasonal stream).'

It turned out that several tourists on their morning safari had spotted a tiger in the Wagahi Nallah. The animal was lying about 20 meters from the road, half-submerged in water, with its head resting on the bank. After observing it for a while, the tourists moved on, assuming it was resting. However, Tulshi noticed that the tiger hadn't flicked its ears even once. Suspecting something was amiss, he borrowed a tourist's binoculars and looked closer. The tiger's chest wasn't rising and falling—no sign of breathing. Observing more closely, he saw its tongue hanging out of its mouth. He realized that something was wrong. Tulshi immediately instructed the driver to head towards Tadoba Lake to alert the forest department.

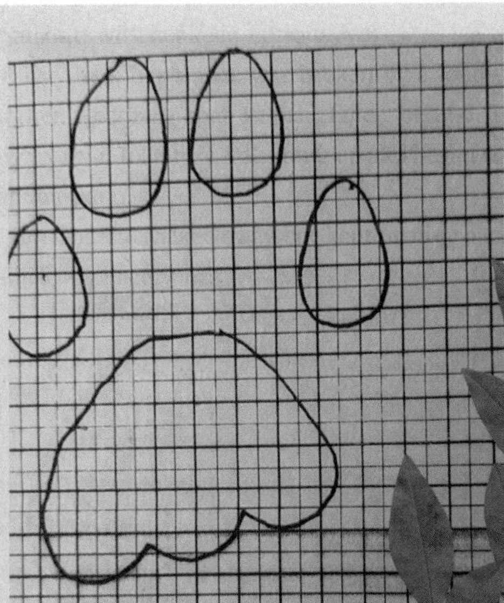

Inked paw print of the tigress Leela

'Oh my God ...' exclaimed Nibuddhe, as he rushed towards the nallah with his team. It was 7.21 a.m. They knew a spot on the way where they would get mobile network coverage, so they paused there briefly to inform the round officer of the Tadoba range about the incident.

By 7.45, Nibuddhe and his colleagues had reached the nallah in Compartment 95 of Kolara. The sight they witnessed left them breathless. The lifeless body of a tiger was wedged between a cluster of bamboo and paper flower thickets. Its head rested on the bank while its hind legs were submerged in water. As they approached, they realized it was a tigress.

Regaining his composure, Nibuddhe immediately called his superiors to give them the update. He warned his team not to touch the body and instructed them to survey the surrounding area. Meanwhile, he took out a GPS device to record the exact location. The team found pugmarks of the tigress in the stream, which they traced carefully. There was no sign of any trap or weapon.

Soon, the field director, deputy directors of the core and buffer zones, other officers, and witnesses arrived at the scene. Veterinarians Dr P. D. Kadukar, Dr Sandeep Chhaukar and Dr Sachin Hagwane were also present. The bamboo and paper flower thickets were cleared, and the tigress's body was moved to an open area. The veterinarians, wearing gloves, first examined her teeth, claws, whiskers and other vital organs to ensure nothing was amiss. They photographed and documented every detail. Age: approximately five to seven years. Length: 170 cm. Tail length: 93 cm. Height: 110 cm. Girth: 120 cm. Impressions of her hind paws were taken using ink.

The postmortem began. The veterinarians made a clean incision on her abdomen and pulled out the intestines. They carefully collected small tissue samples from her liver, lungs, heart and other critical organs, placing them in plastic jars. A total of ten samples were taken, and each jar was labelled immediately.

The officers and staff watched the entire process in stunned silence. But everyone's eyes welled up with tears when the veterinarians pulled out four cubs from her womb—three males and one female. The tigress had been pregnant.

That day, Tadoba lost five tigers.

The postmortem revealed that the tigress had died 10 to 12 hours earlier, between midnight and 1 a.m. Blood clots in her body indicated that she had succumbed to a snakebite.

By 3.20 p.m., all formalities, including the preparation of a panchnama (official report), were completed. In the meantime, forest labourers had gathered wood from East Indian satinwood and Indian boxwood trees and built a pyre. The tigress was cremated there. The entire scene was documented and the cremation was carried out with due process. Afterwards, everyone departed with heavy hearts.

The next day, on 28 October 2012, newspapers carried the headline: 'Tadoba Tigress Leela Dies of Snakebite.'

The Birth of the Queen

The Courting Pair—Leela and Hilltop Male

TADOBA HAS UNDERGONE A SIGNIFICANT TRANSFORMATION OVER THE YEARS. In earlier days, visitors were allowed to go on safaris in private vehicles. Until 2008, the forest department ran a canteen near Tadoba Lake, where tourists gathered for breakfast and exchanged stories of their sightings. Across the road, perched atop a small hill, the forest department's rest house offered overnight stays—one I was fortunate enough to experience. From its veranda, I could gaze across the vast Tadoba Lake. Animals and birds grazing along the lakeside were a common sight there; sometimes, a grey-headed fish eagle carved circles above in search of prey.

One summer, I stayed at that rest house. During the morning safari, other tourists had spotted the tigress that I desperately wished to see. Seeing their photos left me feeling deflated. That afternoon, drawn by frustration, I ventured out alone. Descending the hill, I reached the lake's edge. The place was utterly deserted. Gentle ripples lapped softly at the shore.

Then, I don't know what happened—perhaps the hot wind heightened a slowly building unease—but the stillness suddenly became overwhelming. The realization hit me: I, a young, thin man, with no experience in the wild, was alone in tiger territory. The sheer intensity of that thought sent a chill through me like nothing I had ever felt before. I quickly turned back and hurried to the rest house without looking back.

Those were different times. Around 2010, the Tadoba-Andhari Tiger Reserve, along with the forests of Central Chanda, Brahmapuri and Chandrapur—covering a total of 3,241 square kilometres—was home to approximately sixty-six to seventy-four tigers. Spotting a tiger in Tadoba was not as easy as it is today. Yet, some die-hard visitors would show up season after season. They still do, though the landscape now holds more than 250 tigers today.

Back then, the area surrounding the Tadoba Lake, the twin waterholes of Pandharpauni, a waterhole in Compartment 97, and the Jamunjhora stream flowing through groves of java or black plum trees, was ruled by a tigress. The local guides lovingly called her Leela. Some claimed her name was Neera, but we will stick with Leela. Before Leela's mother, Bandi—or Katrina, as some said—reigned. Bandi had a broken tail, which earned her the name. Her rule lasted only two years, before Leela took over as queen of the area.

Leela soon bonded with a massive male tiger, who resided on a small hill by the road leading to Jamni. He was called the Hilltop Male. In early September 2010, tourists spotted Leela and the Hilltop Male together, deeply engaged in courtship. On 5 September, visitors even witnessed their mating.

When a tigress successfully mates, she becomes pregnant and gives birth after 102 to 108 days. As her pregnancy progresses, her belly becomes round and her pace slows down slightly. Yet, she continues to patrol her territory and hunt to satiate her hunger. When the time comes, she gives birth to two to five cubs (three on average). Newborns weigh between 785 and 1,610 grams and, like kittens, are born with closed eyes that open after six to twelve days. Gaining full vision takes another two weeks. For the first two to three months, they survive solely on their mother's milk. During this time, the tigress constantly moves them to different hiding spots to keep them safe from predators—other tigers, leopards, wild dogs, hyenas, jackals and wolves. Once the cubs are slightly older than three months, she begins bringing back prey for them. Gradually, she takes them along on hunts as they grow up. Male cubs typically leave their mother at around eighteen to twenty-four months to establish their own territory. Female cubs may stay with her until they are twenty to twenty-eight months old before becoming independent.

Leela's union with the Hilltop Male was successful, and in December, she gave birth to four cubs—three females and one male. It's difficult to pinpoint the exact birthdate of tiger cubs in the wild, as tigresses usually retreat to a dense, secluded spot in the forest to give birth and keep the cubs safe from danger. It was only when the cubs were about three months old that Leela brought them out into the open. And that's when the tourists and forest officials saw them for the first time.

At that time, no one knew that one of those cubs would become the undisputed queen of Tadoba, placing this forest firmly on the global wildlife map.

Childhood

P2 with her mother, Leela

In the wild, a male tiger's domain usually includes three or four tigresses, each ruling her own territory. The male visits them in turn, mates and protects them and their cubs from rival males. He visits each tigress alternately, his presence in the lives of these cubs are limited to these brief encounters. It thus falls entirely on the tigress to raise them. She hunts for them, teaches them to hunt and protects them from predators.

Leela had become a mother for the second time. The cubs, around three to three and a half months old, were bundles of energy and mischief. They followed her everywhere, tumbling over each other in constant play. If Leela lay down to rest, they gleefully jumped on her with joy. When exhausted by their antics, she would growl at them in protest—only to pull them in moments later and lick them lovingly. Even in her sleep, her attention was always on the cubs. She would growl softly if any of the cubs wandered out of her sight during play, drawing them back to her side.

When Leela went hunting, she hid the cubs in a secure spot. After a successful hunt, she returned and called them with a soft, distinctive sound. The cubs, who waited all that time, would respond with high-pitched squeals and burst into view. Leela would sit nearby and watch them affectionately as they feasted on the kill.

Since Leela's territory was within the tourist zone, visitors often got a glimpse of her playful brood. The guides, ever practical, named the female cubs P1, P2 and P3, to identify them easily. The male cub was extremely shy and timid, always sticking close to the safety of his mother's side and rarely venturing far from her. His nervous disposition earned him the nickname 'Pandu', a Marathi word used to describe someone who is timid and lacks confidence. Among the sisters, P2 stood out. Bold, mischievous and curious, she strayed from her mother whenever she could. Even the tourist vehicles did not faze her. If an unexpected sound startled the cubs during their playtime, Pandu would quickly run back to his mother while P2 would hold her ground, trying to figure out the source of the noise. They loved to splash around in the water at Pandharpauni, the 97 waterhole, or Ainbodi—a waterhole surrounded by crocodile bark trees. P2 was always the most playful of them all, the ringleader bossing her siblings around. If the others were busy enjoying the water, P2 would sneak up from behind and grab one of their tails in her mouth, pulling it playfully. If a sibling sat still for too long, she'd pounce on them. Even then, the signs of P2's feisty personality were already visible.

The Curious One

The ever-curious P2, always seeking something new

P2 WAS GROWING UP FAST. Alongside her siblings, her inquisitive nature blossomed. She was curious about everything new. The slightest movement in the grass would immediately send her bounding off to investigate. Her mother often scolded her for these antics, occasionally delivering a gentle swipe with her paw. P2 would then sit quietly in one spot for a while, sulking, only to resume her mischief soon after. Her childlike curiosity often gave others around her a scare.

One such incident occurred when Leela's cubs were around eight to nine months old. A group of doctors were travelling from Moharli to Alizanja for a medical camp. Along the way, their guide decided to take a detour to Pandharpauni, hoping to spot a tiger near the waterhole. To their delight, they sighted Leela and her four cubs relaxing in the water at Pandharpauni-2, one of the two waterholes in Pandharpauni area. Seeing five tigers together thrilled the doctors—but the mood shifted quickly. Leela rose from the water and began moving towards Pandharpauni-1, away from the vehicle. The three cubs followed her closely.

One cub, however, stayed behind—intrigued by the unexpected visitors. That cub was P2. For a few moments, she stared intently at the vehicle. Then, with a quiet confidence, she rose from the water and began walking directly towards it. The doctors started feeling uneasy, but the guide reassured them. By then, P2 had reached the road. She circled the vehicle once, examining it closely. The doctors sat frozen, hearts pounding, afraid of what would happen next. She made another round, then settled right in front of the vehicle. There was no aggression in her body language, only childlike curiosity. But that very curiosity sent shivers down the spines of the unprepared guests. Unfazed, P2 continued to observe the vehicle and its wide-eyed occupants with her keen, curious eyes.

Just then, her trance was broken by a loud call. It was her mother. Realizing that P2 had fallen behind, Leela let out a mighty roar. Instantly, P2 sprang up and began trotting towards Pandharpauni-1.

Even as she walked away, she kept turning back to look at the vehicle—still curious.

The Hunt of a Stork

THE YOUNG SIBLINGS WERE GROWING UP UNDER THE PROTECTION OF THEIR MOTHER, LEELA. Occasionally, their father, Hilltop Male, would make an appearance. The cubs would cautiously approach him at first, but once reassured, they would leap onto him playfully. Of course, they felt safest with their mother. When Leela was around, they were at ease. In her absence, they huddled together in hiding, tucked away at the spot she had chosen for them.

As the cubs neared their first year, Leela started taking them along for hunts. Initially, she would leave them hidden in the grass or under a tree while she stalked her prey—teaching by example, she allowed them to learn the intricacies of the hunt. The cubs observed their mother—how she scanned the terrain, identified her prey, locked her gaze on the target, crouched stealthily, then crept forward and pounced at the right moment to overpower her target. Over time, the cubs began participating

Curious, bold and aggressive P2 with her mother

in the hunts. Their youthful impatience often got the better of them; one of them would often rush in too soon, causing the prey to escape. But this, too, was an essential part of their learning process—learning both what to do and what not to do.

By the time P2 and her siblings, including Pandu, were around a year and a half old, they had nearly grown to their mother's size. They started venturing out on their own, making attempts at hunting. Most attempts ended in failure, but with each one, they gained experience.

One February morning in 2012, this family of five was resting comfortably in the grass near the edge of Pandharpauni-2. The yellowish tinge of the grass made it easy for the tigers to blend in. Not far away, seven lesser adjutant storks were perched on a tamarind tree. These were no ordinary birds—about as tall as a tiger, around 110 centimetres, and weighing nearly six kilograms. After a while, the storks took flight and headed towards the waterhole. Just as they were about to land, one of the cubs launched into the air, paws outstretched and grabbed a stork mid-flight. Startled by the sudden attack, the remaining storks flapped furiously into the sky, screeching loudly.

A little later, P2 emerged from the grass, proudly carrying the large stork in her mouth!

The Mischief-Maker

While the cubs were being trained to hunt, their playful mischief was far from over—especially for P2, who was always up to something. Restless by nature, she constantly played pranks on her siblings, often driving her siblings to the brink of irritation.

Even the forest staff weren't spared from her antics.

Every year, Buddha Purnima—the birth anniversary of Lord Gautam Buddha—is a very special night in the forest. It marks the first full moon of the Hindu calendar month Vaishakha. On this night, forest personnel take positions on watchtowers near waterholes to monitor and record animal activity. That year, a few staff members were stationed at a machan (a watchtower made of wood and iron used for wildlife observation) near Ainbodi. There was a mahua tree standing about five feet away from the structure. Around 6 to 6.15 in the evening, Leela arrived at the waterhole with her cubs. After drinking, they settled down to rest—everyone, that is, except P2! True to form, she was drawn to the machan. She circled it a couple of times, while the forest staff above watched her in amusement. But then she began climbing the nearby mahua tree. Panic spread through the machan. The staff decided to radio their superiors for help. By then, P2 had already climbed about seven feet—just five more, and she would have reached the platform. Just then, a well-timed call from Leela broke her focus. P2 abandoned her climb and came down. The team on the machan heaved a collective sigh of relief.

On another day, several tourist vehicles had stopped in the forest at a clearing. A forest guard dismounted from his motorcycle to guide the vehicles into proper formation to prevent crowding. Meanwhile, P2 emerged from the bushes behind

P2 inspecting the forest guard's motorcycle

the vehicles. Despite the presence of all the tourist vehicles, she showed no signs of fear. With a calm, confident stride, she crossed the road and approached the parked motorcycle. Tourists gasped in amazement at her boldness. The forest guard, however, quickly took cover in a nearby Gypsy. P2 was unfazed. Her eyes lit up when she saw the motorcycle—it was something new, something to explore. She sniffed around and noticed a small object dangling from the handlebar: the guard's lunchbox. Her eyes gleamed again, her mischievous streak kicking in. She deftly grabbed the lunchbox with her teeth and trotted off with it as if collecting a toll from those trespassing in her territory. It wouldn't be the last time, either—on two more occasions, she snatched lunchboxes from unsuspecting forest guards.

Yet the staff couldn't help but admire her playful nature. They had begun to realize that this tigress was unlike any other they had known. Photographers and tourists, too , were enchanted by her. Even at such a young age, she seemed to pose fearlessly for the camera.

The same cub would later became known across the world as 'Maya'. How she got that name is a story in itself—but for now, let's just call her Maya.

The First Step

The summer of 2012 was unforgiving. On the last day of May, Maya had started to move through the jungle on her own, away from her mother and siblings. That afternoon, with the heat pressing down she made her way to the Ambepat waterhole in the Pandharpauni area. After drinking, she slipped in the cool water and settled in.

As evening approached, the sun dipped towards the horizon. But Maya showed no inclination to leave. She noticed a tourist jeep parked on the far side of the waterhole but paid it no attention. The visitors watched her, cameras clicking, as she remained still, unbothered by her surroundings.

Then suddenly, her calm demeanour shifted. Maya stirred.

From the opposite direction, a large wild boar had begun to approach the waterhole. Maya lifted her head, glanced at it briefly, then crouched in the water until her body was flat against the ground. She had seen her mother make the same movement while hunting. Now, she was trying it herself. The tourists, who were watching, held their breath. But the boar kept advancing, oblivious to the looming danger. Maya held her position in the water, not a twitch of an ear. Her eyes stayed locked on her target. As the boar got within striking distance, she sprang up from the water. A sudden burst, followed by a spray of water—and the next instant, she was on the boar's back. Realizing what had happened, the animal let out a desperate squeal and tried to throw her off with a violent jolt. But Maya's grip was unshakable. Sharp claws dug in. Teeth sank into the upper part of its neck. The boar fought back with all its might, lifting its body off the ground, but Maya used her weight to pin it down again.

The boar's grunts echoed through the Ambepat area. This

Waiting for the right moment

A sudden strike on the prey

Mounted on the boar's back

Maya had the upper hand from the very first move

Determination versus brute strength

Her first major hunt

was far from an evenly matched contest. The boar was fully grown, powerful and experienced, while Maya, barely a year and a half old, was small and inexperienced. She couldn't figure out how to land a decisive bite on its throat, but she was relentless. The boar kept struggling to break free, and she tightened her hold with each attempt. It became a battle between the boar's brute strength and Maya's unyielding determination. A cloud of dust swirled around them. At one point, the boar managed to rise to all fours, with Maya clinging to its back with all four paws. Just when it seemed the boar might prevail, Maya summoned her strength, and with a fierce thrust slammed its body back to the ground.

Half an hour passed. Both animals were exhausted. Blood trickled from the boar's back, and a large chunk of its neck had been torn. Yet it continued to resist, while Maya remained steadfast, unwilling to let go of her prize. She didn't know precisely how to kill it, but was determined not to lose her hunt.

The fight had lasted a gruelling 45 minutes. As the tourists' safari neared its end, they had to leave the scene. The boar's efforts were weakening; Maya's resolve remained strong. In a decisive moment, she flipped it over like a seasoned wrestler and finally managed to grip its throat. Maya had emerged victorious.

This was possibly her first major solo kill. The intense encounter revealed her aggression, determination and courage—traits that set her apart from her siblings.

Most importantly, it marked the first step in her journey towards becoming the queen of Tadoba.

Orphaned

The monsoon of 2012 came and went, and on 1 October, a new tourist season began. Visitors flocked to Tadoba in large numbers. Leela's cubs were now around twenty-two months old. When the five of them moved together, it was like watching a royal parade—an ambush of tigers. For tourists, it was nothing short of magical.

One day, the family was spotted walking along the Ambepat road. They paused on a small bridge. Leela climbed onto the cement railing. Her two daughters followed and sat beside her. There was hardly any space on the railing for a fourth member, but Maya was unwilling to be left out. She made room for herself by pushing her sisters aside. Poor Pandu stayed below, unable to join.

Just then, the Hilltop Male appeared, giving tourists a rare chance to witness six tigers together.

The cubs still had much to learn from their mother. They would have to part ways in a few short months, leaving their mother behind. But for now, everything seemed secure.

Then, one day, after wandering the forest, the cubs returned and began to search for Leela. They checked the usual spots and called out in plaintive, anxious tones, but there was no response. They were confused and unsettled. Though nearly grown, they were not yet fully independent. They still needed her. But she was nowhere to be found. Exhausted and desperate, they kept searching.

Meantime, by the banks of the Waghai Nallah, Leela's body burned on a funeral pyre.

Like their grandmother Bandi, Leela's time had been cut short. Her sudden death left Maya and her siblings unprepared

The last time the family was seen together

and alone. They hadn't yet mastered the skills of hunting. Feeding four tigers in the wild was an enormous challenge. With each passing day, they grew weaker, visibly losing weight. Slowly, they began to drift apart. P1 was the first to leave Pandharpauni, never to be seen again. P3 moved to the buffer zone of the reserve and was occasionally sighted there. Pandu withdrew deeper into the non-tourism core area, rarely seen by tourists.

And P2 took over her mother's territory. She inherited the richest stretch in the reserve with no challenger to contest her claim. But the question remained: could she hold it? Some doubted whether she could survive alone. She lacked experience and still struggled to hunt efficiently. How would she manage on her own? Tiger enthusiasts and forest staff were concerned.

The tiger population in Tadoba was on the rise. Competition would be fierce. Maya would soon have to defend her territory from stronger, more experienced rivals. The laws of the jungle are unforgiving—she would have to fight for every inch. She was young and untested. And her trials were just beginning.

Bearing the weight of her new territory
and the loss of her mother

Distraught

When the responsibility of a household suddenly falls on children after the loss of their parents, they often grow up too soon. Something similar happened to Maya. After Leela's death, she seemed shaken—a state captured in an incident from January 2013.

One morning, Maya was walking along a road near Tadoba Lake when a langur suddenly emerged from the bushes and stepped on the road, right in front of her. It froze, just 4 or 5 feet away, too stunned to flee. Any tiger would have pounced without hesitation. But Maya seemed distracted. She kept walking, slowly closing the distance. Then something unexpected happened. The langur smacked her across the face. Maya slapped it back.

Distraught after her mother's death

Maya learning about how to become a hunter

The langur, confused, simply sat there. Maya began swatting its face repeatedly with her paw—almost playfully at first. Then she grabbed it by the throat, held it briefly and once it was dead, left the body on the road and continued towards the lake.

How does one interpret this? Why didn't she strike instantly? Was she too inexperienced to hunt properly? Why didn't she eat the kill or even carry it away? Or was she, despite being a tigress, simply moody and prone to eccentricities like a human?

Whatever the reason, this phase didn't last long. Maya soon found her footing. With time, she honed her hunting skills and forged a curious bond with those who followed her journey.

Territory

Tigers are solitary animals, unlike lions, which live in prides. Each tiger carves out its own territory and defends it fiercely. The territory of a male tiger typically spans 60 to 100 square kilometres, while a female's covers around 20 square kilometres. Tigers constantly patrol their areas, marking boundaries by spraying urine on tree trunks and bushes—a behaviour known as 'territory marking'. They also have scent glands near the anus, tail, cheeks and heels, which help reinforce their boundaries.

In addition to scent marking, tigers often rise on their hind legs to scratch tree trunks, leaving deep claw marks. These scent marks and scratches send a clear message to any intruder: back off. A tiger does not tolerate trespassers.

Maya, too, was now the queen of her own territory. She had inherited it from her mother.

It was a prime stretch of forest, ideal for any tiger. Her territory included multiple water sources, most importantly the vast Tadoba Lake. The lake, home to giant crocodiles and abundant fish, also quenched the thirst of animals and birds across the forest. Other waterholes under her control included Pandharpauni-1, Pandharpauni-2, Ainbodi, Compartment 97, Chikhalwahi and Ambepat. Over time, the forest department installed solar-powered pumps to draw water from borewells, ensuring year-round access, even during the height of summer.

These waterholes were surrounded by grasslands or bamboo thickets—ideal for resting, stalking or ambushing prey. Hunting near water was easier than in the open. The grasslands drew species like wild boars, spotted deer, sambar, barking deer and gaur, offering a rich and diverse prey base. What more could a tigre ask for?

A map of Maya's territory

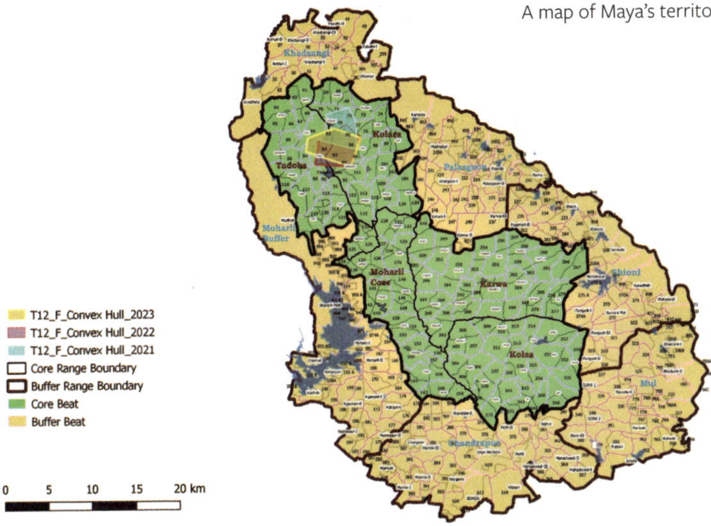

Like any tiger, Maya regularly patrolled her territory. She was often seen marking her scent in key areas like Bhave Bandhara, Chital road, Waghzari, Talav road and others. Significantly, much of her territory fell within the tourism zone. As she moved through her domain to patrol, mark or rest, a convoy of tourist vehicles often followed her during safari hours.

Some parts of Maya's territory overlapped with neighbouring tigresses, leading to occasional minor conflicts. Her neighbours included Babli in the Fasilaga area, the Katezari Female near Bhave Bandhara and Tower road, Sharmili near Gidhad Taka and Choti Tara near Jamunbodi. On Hilltop road, an unusual scene sometimes unfolded—Maya's territory lay on one side of the road and Choti Tara's on the other. Both tigresses would occasionally come to mark their territories at the same time. Maya would walk along one side while Choti Tara walked on the other, either parallel to each other, slightly ahead or behind each other. Yet they rarely tried to trespass into each other's territory or provoke a confrontation. Where did they learn such restraint?

Ironically, after Maya's disappearance, it was Choti Tara who took over her stronghold at Pandharpauni.

Maya marking her territory

The Fawn

Maya tenderly caring for a spotted deer fawn, as if it were her own cub

In November 2013, a curious incident took place.

Early one morning, Maya was patrolling the borders of her territory, marking it as she moved. A convoy of tourist vehicles followed her at a distance. From Jamunbodi, she headed toward Magar Tank (a former crocodile-breeding site) and then slipped into the tall grass, leaving the road behind.

It was nearly 8 a.m. and most tourists assumed she wouldn't return to the road anytime soon. They moved on. But four vehicles, whose occupants had yet to see her, decided to wait, hoping for a glimpse. With Maya out of sight, some photographers turned their attention to an Indian roller bird, perched on a nearby teak tree. Just then, tourists in one of the vehicles noticed something remarkable. They had spotted Maya—and could see clearly what she was doing.

Inside the grass, Maya had come upon a young spotted deer fawn. It was likely the fawn that had drawn her into the grass in the first place. Capturing such a small animal was no challenge for her—with a single leap, she had it. But she didn't kill it.

Instead, she gently held it in her mouth, cradling it almost as if carrying her own cub, taking great care not to injure it with her teeth. Then she delicately placed the fawn in a slight clearing and to everyone's astonishment, started licking it as if she was tenderly grooming her own young! She thoroughly licked and cleaned the fawn, then began to play with it! Each time the fawn tried to run away, Maya gently pinned it down with a paw and continued the game. This playful interaction lasted a full 15 minutes.

Some observers wondered: was this a prelude? Cats often toy with mice before killing them. Was Maya planning to do the same?

But once again, Maya defied expectations. When she was done, she simply let the fawn go. The little one scampered away in search of its mother. Maya, unbothered, moved on and later settled near Panchdhara.

Why did she behave this way? Perhaps her hunger was already satisfied, so she had no interest in hunting the fawn? But if that were the case, what explained the affection—the grooming, the play?

Although Maya's popularity among tourists rose each day by this time, incidents such as this confused even the most seasoned tiger experts.

The First Casualty

9 JANUARY 2014. It was 11 a.m. The winter air still held a chill. Safari hours had ended, the tourist vehicles had departed and the jungle had settled back into its usual calm. Animals and birds rested in their hidden shelters, and the forest was quiet once again.

But in one corner, a steady thud-thud sound broke this silence. Behind the Ainbodi waterhole in Kolara, a few men were illegally chopping bamboo. In the core area of the forest, no human activity is permitted except for limited tourism and forest department duties. These men knew they weren't supposed to be there.

Suddenly, a scream tore through the air, sending a chill down everyone's spines. It was Vitthal Nagoshe, one of the trespassers. Out of nowhere, a tiger had attacked him. Before anyone could comprehend what was happening, the tiger had killed him and started dragging his body away. Terrified, the others fled through the bamboo thickets and immediately alerted the forest department.

Officials promptly arrived at Ainbodi and launched a search operation, following the drag marks left by the tiger. Before long, they found a severed human leg. The trail led to a grassy patch where it abruptly ended, indicating that the tiger had hidden the body there. But the grass was too dense and dangerous to enter. The search had to pause.

Using binoculars, they spotted a tiger sitting in the grass. It was then that everyone realized that the tiger responsible for Nagoshe's death was none other than Maya! She was unwilling to let go of the body. Whenever the forest personnel attempted to approach, she growled menacingly, clearly not ready to surrender. Given the risk, the decision was unanimously made not to go near her.

In the end, Nagoshe's family carried back only his severed leg, which was cremated. The forest department provided ₹35,000 for the funeral expenses. No financial assistance was granted. According to regulations, financial assistance is not offered when a person is attacked by a wild animal while illegally entering the core area of the jungle. Perhaps that's why this incident did not gain much attention.

The conclusion drawn was simple—Maya had attacked and killed a human, who had illegally trespassed into her territory.

Bold and Beautiful

The Queen of Pandharpauni earned the name 'Maya' in 2013. The once-mischievous cub had grown into a confident tigress. Her popularity had soared to the point where it rivalled that of film stars. Whenever she walked along the forest roads, tourist vehicles lined up in front and behind her. It became a common sight: Maya walking with quiet authority while her fans followed in tow. At times, she would pass so close to a vehicle that one could almost reach out and touch her. Occasionally, she would pause and lock eyes directly with someone, causing hearts to skip a beat. Much like a celebrity striking a pose for the cameras, Maya often paused mid-walk, with a picture-perfect pose. Wildlife photographers were captivated by her.

Her slightly small eyes became her most recognizable feature.

Around this time, safari guides noticed that the stripes on Maya's left cheek formed a distinctive trident-like pattern. And the markings on her right shoulder resembled the letter 'M'. That's when they gave her the name 'Maya'. With her elegant presence and affectionate nature, the name felt befitting.

By now, Maya had honed her hunting skills. Watching her cautiously move through the golden grass, stalking her prey, was mesmerizing. She would single out the weakest target from a herd of deer or a sounder of wild boars, isolate it and strike with precision. Remarkably, she often hunted in full view of tourists or proudly carried her kill as she walked past them. These bold displays earned her the title: the 'Bold and Beautiful' tigress.

Maya was now three years old, entering a new phase of life. Her territory markings were not only a declaration of her dominance, but also a signal to potential mates. She was ready for motherhood. One such message drifted across Tadoba and

Gabbar, Maya's first partner

reached the keen senses of a male tiger—the robust king of Jamni's grasslands, Gabbar. Just like the infamous character from the Hindi movie *Sholay*, this Gabbar was imposing and unmissable. He became the first hero in Maya's life.

The scent of a tigress in oestrus emits a strong scent through her urine and it uses unique mating to calls attract a male. In response, the male also makes distinctive calls to announce his presence. The mating process typically lasts about a week. During this period, the pair stays together, mating frequently, then resting.

They communicate with each other through specific vocalizations. During mating, their behaviour exhibit both aggression and play. The male mounts the female from behind, sometimes biting her neck, while the female may swipe at him playfully in response. Their interactions often look like a playful tussle.

A queen in her element—
Maya, with the aura of a
screen legend

In mid-February 2014, tourists witnessed the mating pair Maya and Gabbar together. By late April, Maya's movements had slowed down.

In May, she disappeared from public view.

First-Time Mother

In late May 2014, Maya gave birth to two cubs. Her admirers were overjoyed—it felt as though two new members had joined their own families. It was her first time as a mother. What did Maya's cubs look like? Only the forest staff knew, but Maya, as always, soon revealed the secret herself.

Though it was already monsoon season, the rains had yet to arrive. On 10 June 2014, by 8.30 in the morning, the air was thick and hot. Around forty safari vehicles were stationed at Panchdhara, all eagerly waiting for a glimpse of Maya. Half an hour to 45 minutes passed. Only a few deer, monkeys and mongoose had approached the water. Still, no sign of Maya. Then, a team of forest personnel arrived. The staff got out of their vehicle and started patrolling the left side of the road. They walked towards the water. Barely 2 minutes later, a distinct alarm call of a sambar rang out from the other side. It was a signal that Maya was nearby. The patrolling team quickly returned to their vehicle. By now, the excitement among the tourists had peaked. Everyone stood alert on tiptoes, eyes wide open in anticipation.

After a few seconds of suspense, Maya made her grand entrance before the crowd of her admirers. She came walking calmly from the direction of the sambar's alarm call. Her walk had its usual grace, but today, she paid no heed to her fans. She continued walking towards the water on the left side, where the patrol team had just gone.

Some people could still see her as she moved towards the bushes near the water. Once there, she picked something up in her mouth. People tried to see through binoculars and camera lenses, but it wasn't clear. The visitors speculated: 'It's a rabbit', 'She has caught a mongoose.'

The first-time mother, carefully relocating one of her cubs to a safer place

Maya sat in the water for about 10 to 15 minutes. Everyone held their breath, waiting. Suddenly, someone whispered, 'She's getting up, she's getting up.' Maya rose from the water and started walking out slowly. As usual, a cheer of admiration rose from the crowd—but this time, it was accompanied by gasps of surprise and joy. The spectators could hardly believe their eyes—Maya was carrying a tiny cub in her mouth.

The cub was barely ten to twelve days old! Maya's powerful jaws, capable of killing sambars and crushing bone, now appeared as gentle as rose petals. She held the cub like it was made of glass. Right there, in front of hundreds of astonished onlookers, Maya was relocating her cubs, one by one, to a safer den. Cameras clicked non-stop as she cautiously walked past the vehicles. On the way, she paused twice to scan the surroundings for any threats. Then she continued towards Magar Tank, disappearing behind it and out of sight.

For Maya's fans who witnessed it, this moment felt transcendent. People high-fived, hugged, even wiped tears of joy from their eyes. It was as if they had shared a sacred moment.

Unfortunately, this joy was not to last for long.

Tragedy

Grief in motion: Maya wanders the forest, looking for her lost cubs

Shortly after Maya proudly presented her cubs to her fans, a tragic incident occurred, forcing her to confront misfortune once again.

One morning, a pack of ten to twelve wild dogs was seen moving along the Chital road—a favourite haunt of spotted deer. The land on either side of this road was full of stones, and hence provided a great camouflage for spotted deer. Hence, herds of spotted deer visited this road regularly to rest.

Wild dogs, or dholes, are social animals that live and hunt in packs. The alpha male and female lead the group, with the other members following their commands. Their unique hunting style involves surrounding a prey from all sides as they communicate with each other through whistle-like sounds. Once the prey is exhausted from running, the dholes close in and attack. Unlike other predators, they do not suffocate their prey; instead, they begin tearing it apart while it's still alive. This behaviour makes them seem brutal, despite their otherwise domestic dog-like appearance. But to describe them using traits like brutality or savagery is to project human emotion onto an animal following its instincts.

That morning, as the wild dogs walked along the Chital road, tourists watched and photographed them with fascination. All of a sudden, Maya appeared. The mood of the tourists' beloved tigress instantly changed upon seeing the wild dogs. No tigress, especially a nursing mother, can tolerate the presence of wild dogs in her territory, as they pose a threat to her offspring. The moment she spotted the pack, she charged at them. Chaos erupted. The dogs' high-pitched yelps echoed through the area. Although smaller than Maya, the dogs had strength in numbers and stood their ground. But Maya wasn't deterred. Roaring, she attacked any dog within reach even as they tried to encircle her. In the commotion, she swiftly struck one with her paw, instantly knocking it down, then clamped its throat and ended its struggle. Moments later, she brought down a second. Despite the loss of two pack mates, the remaining wild dogs continued the fight. However, within minutes, Maya claimed a third victim. This was enough to break the pack's morale. The sight of the enraged mother was too much to face. The dogs fled. Maya picked up one of the dead dogs and headed towards Magar Tank, where her cubs were hidden.

Tragically, within two days of this incident, the lifeless bodies of the cubs were found. In all likelihood, they had been killed by the same wild dogs.

After their death, Maya was devastated. She wandered through the forest for days, searching and calling for them. She didn't understand what had happened. Watching her in this state brought tears to the eyes of her admirers. Neither Maya nor her fans knew that this was not the end, but only the beginning of her hardships.

T12

The 'M' on her shoulder made her 'Maya' to the world, but to the forest staff she was 'T12'

The name 'Maya', derived from the M-shaped pattern on her right shoulder, perfectly matched her affectionate nature. However, in 2014, Maya was officially assigned the identification number T12.

But how are such IDs assigned to tigers?

The forest department gives each identified tiger a unique

number, and these IDs are the only official records maintained in the departmental documents. The forest department never gives names to tigers. Instead, it is the safari guides and Gypsy drivers who assign the animals easy-to-remember names based on their appearance, behaviour, personality, the area they inhabit or distinctive stripe patterns. For example, another famous tigress, Sonam was named for the S shaped pattern on her body. These names, while widely used and beloved by tourists, remain unofficial.

Every year, the forest department conducts a large-scale camera trapping operation in the forest. Thousands of photos are captured and analyzed during this process. Newly identified tigers are assigned official IDs—but only adult tigers receive official permanent IDs. Cubs and younger sub-adults are excluded.

There are two main criteria to give a permanent ID: the tiger must be more than two years old or it must have separated from its mother, even if it is under two years of age. For instance, if a tiger is eighteen months old but has become independent, it receives an ID—even if it still resides within its mother's territory. Similarly, if it is two years old but still lives with its mother, it is given an ID, as it is classified as an adult.

Over the past few decades, camera traps equipped with infrared sensors and motion detectors have become a cornerstone of wildlife conservation. With minimal human intervention, they allow extensive wildlife research and reveals numerous secrets about animal behaviour. These cameras are typically installed around one-and-a-half to two feet off the ground on roads, dirt tracks, trails, dry streams, riverbeds and waterholes frequented by the animals.

They have proved particularly vital in tiger conservation. Previously, tiger population surveys relied on observations from machans or pugmark tracking. Now, camera trapping provides far more accurate counts. Cameras are placed on both sides of paths frequently used by tigers, so that photos can be captured from both sides, as is necessary for identification. Just like fingerprints in humans, each tiger has a unique black stripe pattern on its body. By analyzing these patterns, researchers can determine whether the tiger has been previously recorded. If yes, the existing ID is retained. If not, the tiger is given the next available ID number in sequence.

Through this process, Maya was officially assigned the ID 'T12'. But for her admirers, she would always be 'Maya'.

Beloved

Maya's affectionate nature made her a favourite among the forest staff. It was rare to find a gathering without someone bringing her up. Everyone had a personal story or an encounter to share—and she was considered an integral member of the Tadoba family.

Even today, when I meet current or former employees from the Tadoba and Kolara ranges, the topic of Maya naturally comes up in conversation. Those who had seen her since her cub days often say, 'Maya's behaviour was so friendly, we used to forget that she was a tigress.' Forest workers frequently encounter tigers and other wild animals while working in the jungle—Maya was no exception—but she never attacked any of them. On some occasions, she even came within just two to five feet. Yet, she never showed any aggression.

In the past, there was a colony for forest workers near Tadoba Lake. Maya never caused any trouble there. Once, while walking along the road near the colony, a crowd gathered to catch a glimpse of her. Maya calmly sat down under a tree just 5 feet from the crowd. People stood and watched her with fascination. Then, without a warning she let out a mild growl. Instantly, the crowd scattered in panic. People ran towards their homes; a few fell in the commotion as others stumbled over them in the rush. Maya, on the other hand, stayed where she was, watching the spectacle—almost as if amused. To this day, the workers who ran away in fear can't help but laugh when they recall that incident.

Though the colony was eventually vacated, the forest rest house near the lake still stands. The quarters for the watchmen and forest rest house staff is nearby. Maya often roamed around the rest house. Sometimes, she would sit beside the fence. Even

Maya and the villagers:
a rare coexistence

then, she never attempted to intrude. On occasion, she would glance at the staff taking photos of her on their phones from behind the fence—then continue on her way.

One day, Rama Warbhe, the most senior and experienced forest worker, was at the rest house. He saw Maya walking near the fence and assumed she might head towards the lake. After some time, he stepped outside with two colleagues. What he didn't realize was that Maya was sitting close by. As soon as she saw the three of them, she sprinted in their direction. Alarmed, Rama and his companions quickly took shelter inside the yard of their quarters. Maya had very come close by now. She stopped, looked at them for a moment, then headed towards the lake. Clearly, it was not an attack but a warning.

Reflecting on the incident, Rama admitted honestly, 'Maya

The beloved tigress of the forest workers

taught us a lesson that day because we stepped out carelessly.'

At that time, the Kolsa, Palasgaon and Ran Talodhi villages had not been relocated outside the core area. Villagers travelled by motorcycles through forest roads, sometimes with women and children. At times, they encountered Maya. If she was

walking down the road, the villagers would stop their vehicles and let her pass. Sometimes, she changed her path to avoid them. Other times, she kept walking ahead while the villagers followed her at a safe distance on their motorcycles.

Not once did she attack.

The Stakeholders

At 97 waterhole, Maya mates with Gabbar

In 2015, Maya and Gabbar were seen together again, raising hopes that she might become a mother for the second time. However, this time something unusual occurred. Gabbar was no longer the only male tiger in her territory. Two others—Navegaon Male and Namdev—had also entered her domain.

Everyone was baffled to see Maya mating with all three of them. What did it mean for a tigress mate with three different males?

By June or July, Maya gave birth to three cubs—two males and one female. Determining which of the three males fathered the litter was difficult, though some guides speculated that Namdev was most likely the father. It was certain that the other two males posed a threat to the cubs. Male tigers are known to kill cubs that are not their own, both to establish their own lineage and to bring the tigress back into heat, giving them a chance to sire their offspring. Maya was now faced with the challenge of protecting her cubs from any male who wasn't their father.

Even as she balanced the demands of motherhood and fended off increasing pressure from these male tigers, Maya continued to play her part in keeping Tadoba in the limelight. Despite the turmoils in her life, she remained a favourite among tourists. Her cubs, like their mother, were bold and unafraid—delighting visitors and photographers alike.

The antics of Maya and her cubs drew more tourists to Tadoba. Now, multiple male tigers could be spotted in the same territory, making sightings more exciting. It turned many visitors into regulars at the reserve. However, the presence of multiple males was a growing stress for Maya. Even after giving birth, she was seen mating with them. Some experts believed that this was a strategic act—Maya was 'fake mating' to deceive the tigers and keep them away from her cubs. For the first time, this behaviour was discussed as a possible evolutionary tactic.

But why were so many male tigers drawn to Maya's territory? The answer lay in the area's richness. With ample water sources and a thriving prey base, her territory was a paradise for carnivores. Every tiger wanted a share. Also with increasing population, the density of tigers in Tadoba was increasing.

One might ask—if Maya was so fierce, why didn't she fight off these males? At times, she did. But most of the time, she couldn't succeed. The reason lay in biology. The male tigers are naturally larger and stronger than females. In the Royal Bengal Tiger species, a male typically measures between 270 and 310 cm; females, between 240 and 265 cm. Tail lengths range from 85 to 110 cm for both sexes. But in weight, the difference is stark. Males weigh between 175 to 260 kg, while females weigh only 100 to 160 kg. At her strongest, therefore, a female tiger weighs just as much as the smallest male.

How could she ever hope to match a male in a fight?

Fearless and Bold

On 23 October 2015, Maya proudly introduced her new cubs to tourists near Pandharpauni. Her fans were overjoyed once again. She stayed with her tiny cubs around the Pandharpauni area, who—much like their mother—were fearless and bold from the start. They played openly in front of the tourist vehicles, drawing a surge of photographers to Tadoba hoping to capture these moments. The fame of Maya, her cubs and Tadoba had spread far and wide.

On the morning of 22 November, Maharashtra's then chief minister, Devendra Fadnavis, visited the reserve. When he reached Pandharpauni, Maya, like an excellent host, appeared to greet him. She walked from Pandharpauni to Tadoba Lake with her five- to six-month-old cubs. This time, she surprised everyone: midway through her 'roadshow', she paused to pick up one of the cubs in her mouth. No one had seen a tigress carry a cub that old before. Perhaps that cub was slightly weaker, prompting Maya to carry it for part of the way. But the surprises didn't stop there. Maya went on to display her hunting prowess right in front of the chief minister. She skilfully hunted a sambar deer and, with ease and grace, dragged her kill behind a tree. The chief minister was left speechless—awed by her majestic aura and dominance.

Later that same day, former Indian spinner and wildlife photographer Anil Kumble went on a safari. Maya and her cubs made an appearance again, generously allowing him the opportunity to capture a series of stunning photographs.

Maya's first litter had not survived. So, this was the first generation of her cubs that the public could watch thrive. The affection they inspired was immense. With their fearless energy, everyone agreed—they were truly Maya's offspring.

Maya's cubs frolicking at Pandharpauni

Maya and her three cubs

Immortal

Maya with her cub in an embrace

MAYA HAD LONG BEEN A FAVOURITE AMONG WILDLIFE PHOTOGRAPHERS. She rarely disappointed, allowing striking images to be captured effortlessly. Her photos created waves on social media and frequently featured in newspapers. Maya brought not only joy, but fame and fortune to many photographers. One such

Maya and her cub, immortalized on a postage stamp

opportunity came to Amol Bais, a photographer from Chandrapur.

On the morning of 6 January 2016, Maya was resting leisurely on the Pandharpauni road. The soft morning sunlight enhanced her radiant appearance. One of her cubs was playing beside her—biting her tail or nipping at her. Whenever the cub strayed a little too far, Maya let out a distinct growl, and the cub would come scampering back, leaping by her side. The air was filled with affection.

As the morning safari began, tourist vehicles arrived, as usual, at what had become known as 'Maya's Darbar', the queen's court. Yet, their presence didn't disturb her tranquillity or the cub's playfulness. Then, in a perfect moment, Maya sat upright and the cub stood on its hind legs, wrapping its front paws around her in a perfect embrace. Amol captured it. He posted the photo on Facebook, where it went viral—quickly amassing over 250 million likes. Praise came in from all over the world. It was featured on the front page of *The Hindu*, as well as in the UK-based newspaper *The Daily Mirror*.

But the magic of Maya and her cub didn't stop there. The image deeply moved Maharashtra's then forest minister, Sudhir Mungantiwar, who proposed that this picture be featured on a postal stamp to mark World Tiger Day. The central government responded swiftly, and on 31 July 2016, a ₹25 stamp bearing the image of Maya and her cub was unveiled at Nagpur's Manakapur Indoor Stadium. The release made headlines again. Soon after, the Nagpur Metro Railway featured the same image on the doors of its trains.

Training

One day in April 2016, Maya was sitting calmly near Pandharpauni-1. Her three cubs were playing nearby. Now ten months old, they were fully immersed in their play. Tourists watched the scene from the road while a lone Indian gaur grazed a short distance from the vehicles. It seemed to be an old female, nearing the end of her prime. Suddenly, Maya's attention shifted toward the gaur. She rose from her spot and slipped into

Learning to kill: Maya's cubs launch an attack on a gaur

the grass. Intuitively, her cubs stopped playing and followed her. The tourists lost sight of all four as they disappeared into the undergrowth.

Moments later, one of the cubs leapt onto the gaur's back. The spectators were stunned by this unexpected move, but the gaur remained unfazed. Could it not feel the cub's weight? Were its claws not sharp enough to pierce the hide? Before these questions could even form fully, a second cub climbed onto the gaur, then the third. All three dug their claws into its back, biting wherever they could. Blood began to flow from the wounds, yet the gaur remained motionless. It could have easily shaken off the cubs with a single jolt or at least have run away. But it did nothing. Why?

The reason was revealed when the gaur collapsed to the ground. Maya had grabbed its hind leg in her jaws and torn the muscles, rendering it immobile. After her cubs mounted the gaur, she stepped back and let them take the lead. Even after the gaur fell, Maya did not go for its throat. She watched as her cubs launched a frenzied attack—biting, clawing, struggling to find the vital spot. Eventually, the wounds took their toll, and the gaur succumbed. The family then feasted together.

Typically, when a tigress teaches her cubs to hunt, she begins with smaller prey like rabbit, monkey or fawn, often bringing them alive. She carries it gently to her cubs, just as she would carry them. The cubs then play with the prey before delivering the fatal bite.

Maya, breaking the usual rules of the tiger kingdom, had chosen a full-grown gaur to train her cubs! Perhaps the queen of Tadoba wanted to raise her cubs to be as fearless and formidable as she was.

The Test

Moment of reckoning: Maya's cubs make their first independent kill—a barking deer

Barely a week after that incident, Maya appeared to set another challenge for her cubs.

The three young tigers were resting in the dense grass on the island at the centre of the Pandharpauni-2. Hidden from view, they lay in wait. After some time, Maya arrived at the waterhole's edge. She drank deeply, then quietly climbed over the mud embankment on the far side and disappeared.

Soon, a cautious barking deer approached from the tree line. After scanning its surroundings and sensing no immediate danger, it drank and then proceeded to move over the embankment, following the same path Maya had taken.

Once the barking deer was out of sight, one of the cubs descended from the island and sat by the waterhole's edge. Everything seemed calm.

Then came a sudden bark—an alarm call from the barking deer, followed by the sound of it racing back at full speed. Just behind it, Maya came charging down at lightning speed, claws extended, her face set in fierce determination. The terrified barking deer splashed into the water, racing towards the side where one of the cubs was already waiting. As soon as it came within reach, the cub leapt. The other two cubs emerged from the grass and pounced on the deer too.

And Maya? She had already stopped. Now she stood still, watching intently to see how her cubs would handle the situation. One cub locked its jaws around the deer's throat while the other two pinned it down from behind. The deer thrashed, trying to escape, but the cubs held firmly. Within seconds, the struggle was over.

Maya approached her cubs slowly. She licked their faces and rubbed against them as if acknowledging that they had passed her test. Then, she quietly moved aside and let them feast on the reward of their hard work.

Wild Dog Hunt

It was a cool September morning in 2016. The monsoon had just ended, leaving the forest at Navegaon lush and green. Spotted deer and sambar grazed on the tender grass in the meadow. Nearby, a sounder of wild boars rooted about, their young piglets in tow. When wild boar piglets are very young, they aren't black like the adults; instead they sport a pale, earthy coat with dark stripes of the same hue. The camouflage blends them seamlessly into the dappled forest floor of dirt and dried leaves. Along the forest paths in Navegaon, tall grass and shrubs had grown, making it easy for a predator to lie in wait unnoticed.

Amidst this setting, a pair of wild dogs casually strolled along the road, absorbed in their courtship. There was no sign of their pack members around; this was likely the alpha pair. Among wild dogs, The alpha female is intensely possessive of their mate. Whenever her mate defecates, she immediately lifts her hind legs high and urinates over the spot, while balancing delicately on her front limbs. This masks the male's scent with her own. And if any other female sniffs the droppings, she only detects a female's scent, preventing her from locating the male.

The female in this pair too performed this ritual. Afterwards, they continued walking, gently brushing each other affectionately as they moved in their characteristic relaxed trot. However, they were oblivious to the danger lurking nearby. Maya lay hidden in the grass, just off the roadside on the left. She had been tracking them from afar, and now waited motionlessly for the perfect moment.

As soon as the wild dogs came within striking distance, she pounced—like a lightning bolt—from the green. With a burst

The wild dog pair, lost in their courtship

Maya, waiting for the right moment

The ambush—Maya launches her sudden attack

One swift, lethal strike ends the chase

A successful hunt

of speed, she launched her attack. The unexpected ambush sent the wild dogs into a frantic panic, their loud yelps shattering the silence in the forest. They tried to escape by turning to flee into the underbrush. One escaped, but its partner wasn't so lucky. With her first leap, Maya took a leap from the grass onto the road, and with her second, she struck the fleeing dog, bringing it down. In the next breath, her jaws sank into its throat and silenced its cries.

The game was over within seconds. Maya proudly picked up her prey and walked past the tourists, disappearing into the jungle.

The Second Casualty

For the forest department, summer is the most demanding time of the year. The scorching heat turns the jungle's grasses dry and yellow. Trees shed their leaves, carpeting the forest floor in a thick layer of dry foliage. Branches become bare and brittle. In Tadoba, dry bamboo leaves scatter everywhere, creating a tinderbox. Under such conditions, a single spark—whether accidental or deliberate—can ignite a wildfire that quickly spreads with the wind. If not contained promptly, hundreds of acres can be reduced to ashes. These fires not only destroy trees and shrubs but also kill millions of insects, thousands of birds along with their eggs and nests, and hundreds of animals, wiping out their habitats. It takes years for such areas to regenerate.

To prevent and manage wildfires, the forest department staff often put their lives on the line. Most wildfires aren't naturally occurring. Many start due to human negligence, or worse, through deliberate acts of arson. The department conducts awareness campaigns in villages near the forest, educating communities about the causes and consequences of wildfires, and warning of legal consequences. Patrolling is intensified to prevent unauthorized entry into the forest. Grass strips are deliberately burned at the start of the summer season to create 'fire lines' that act as barriers to wildfires.

During summer, special fire watchers are appointed, usually from nearby villages. This provides seasonal employment and strengthens community involvement in forest conservation efforts. Fire watchers stay in protection huts built at strategic locations within the forest and keep a round-the-clock vigil. In Tadoba, tall watchtowers offer a sweeping view of the forest, making twenty-four-hour surveillance possible. If smoke is detected anywhere in the forest, the watchtower alerts the fire control room, which immediately relays the information via wireless communication to the nearest protection hut. The fire watchers then rush to the site to extinguish the flames.

In the summer of 2017, three fire watchers—Ratiram Nehare, Shankar Rane and Mangaldas Choudhary—were on duty in the Tadoba range. All three, aged between forty-five and fifty, were residents of Navegaon Ramdegi village in Chimur tehsil. Since 16 February, they had been staying in the quarters near Tadoba Lake. On the morning of 1 May, they woke up as usual and stepped out for their morning routine. It was 5.30 a.m. Summer daylight had already brightened the surroundings. They crossed the road in front of their quarters and stopped about a hundred metres away, in Compartment 95. There, they squatted together along the fire line to relieve themselves. In front of them lay the Tadoba Lake. All was calm, with no signs of danger.

At that same moment, a tiger was making its way from Magar Tank towards the lake. It spotted the three figures on the fire line. Silently, it approached them and suddenly attacked from the left. Mangaldas was caught in its grip. The tiger's canines pierced his neck. As he uttered his last words—'Save me!'—the pressure from the bite crushed his trachea. He died on the spot. Panicked, Ratiram and Shankar screamed to scare the tiger away. But it gave a sharp jerk, lifted Mangaldas's lifeless body and dragged it northward.

In the meantime, hearing the cries, other fire watchers rushed out from their quarters. They alerted the Assistant Fire Protection Officer B. D. Barsagade, who rushed to the scene, along with other officials. A search began for Mangaldas.

About 100 metres away, Mangaldas's body was found face-up among the rocks. His clothes were completely torn. Scanning the area, the team spotted a tiger crouched behind a bush. It was a familiar tigress—Maya.

As the crowd gathered, Maya slipped away. Meanwhile, Mangaldas's family was informed of the tragic incident. The

A visual interpretation of the fatal incident involving Maya

police arrived at the scene, and the body was sent to the sub-district hospital in Chimur. The postmortem report stated that the cause of death was excessive blood loss due to the rupture of the trachea and lungs. The tigress's canines had punctured Mangaldas's neck, tearing both his trachea and oesophagus. A bone near the left side of his neck was fractured, four ribs were broken, and his right lung haemorrhaged.

That evening, Mangaldas's body was cremated in his village. As per government regulations, his wife was granted financial assistance of ₹8 lakh.

And Maya? Her routine continued without any interruptions or changes.

Question Mark

Matkasur, who may have played a role in Mangaldas's death

THIS INCIDENT LEFT MAYA'S ADMIRERS SHOCKED. How could a tigress, known for her friendly demeanour towards tourists, suddenly attack and kill a man dedicated to protecting the forest from wildfires? Has she turned into a man-eater? Were tourists now at risk? These and many other questions swirled in people's minds. But before jumping to conclusions, it's essential to consider some scientific facts.

First, Maya was a wild tigress, not a domesticated house cat. She resided in her natural habitat, and all her instincts were driven by the laws of nature. Despite decades of research on tigers, no one can claim to have unlocked every mystery of their behaviour.

The second fundamental truth is that humans are not natural prey for tigers. In fact, tigers typically avoid humans. They have no inherent interest in us. Instances of tigers turning into man-eaters are exceedingly rare. It usually occurs when a tiger becomes too old, suffers any severe injury, or loses its canines—making it incapable of hunting its usual prey. In such cases, a tiger may target humans. Similarly, a tigress with cubs might attack if a human comes too close, purely to protect her young. But under normal circumstances, a tiger prefers to steer clear of humans.

The forest department repeatedly advises that people avoid sitting or crouching while working in areas frequented by tigers or leopards. If they must do so, someone should stand guard around them. This is because a crouched or seated person appears smaller and could potentially cause a tiger or leopard to mistake them for a deer, wild boar or some other prey. Such confusion can lead to tragic consequences.

Taking these facts into account, the reasoning behind this incident becomes clearer. It also becomes evident that Maya had not turned into a man-eater and that tourists watching her from vehicles were not at risk.

However, some eyewitnesses later shared an intriguing detail with me. Another character may have been involved in this incident. According to them, it wasn't Maya sitting near Mangaldas's body but the male tiger Matkasur. Maya, they said, was nearby—watching from a short distance. Which raises yet another question: who exactly killed Mangaldas—Maya or Matkasur?

Matkasur

Bhola, the lone surviving cub, halts traffic on the Pandharpauni–Navegaon road

AROUND 2016–17, ANOTHER POWERFUL MALE TIGER ENTERED MAYA'S TERRITORY—MATKASUR. With his arrival, Maya's worries escalated. He was extremely aggressive, and Maya avoided direct confrontation with him.

By this time, her cubs were nearly a year old and had started exploring the Pandharpauni area on their own. Once, near Pandharpauni-2, the cubs came face-to-face with Matkasur when Maya wasn't around. Seizing the opportunity, he attacked the cubs. Though the cubs were three in number, his strength was overwhelming. The cubs scattered, desperately seeking cover in the tall grass. But Matkasur pursued them relentlessly.

After that day, two of Maya's cubs were never seen again. It is believed they fell victim to Matkasur's attack. The third cub, later named Bhola, survived. He was occasionally spotted, likely trying to survive by staying out of Matkasur's way. On the rare occasions when Maya stood up to Matkasur, Bhola would join his mother in defence. In late February 2018, Bhola was seen sitting in the middle of the Pandharpauni–Navegaon road. At the time, a state transport bus to Chimur still used that route. Both tourist vehicles and the bus had to halt due to Bhola's 'roadblock'. Eventually, when the bus driver revved the engine, he finally moved away but the onlookers noticed he had an injury on his back. After that incident, Bhola was never seen again. His fate remains unknown.

Meanwhile, Matkasur's presence continued to trouble Maya. She made every effort to avoid him, carefully strategizing her movements. But he pursued her everywhere she went.

Once, Maya was sitting on the road near Pandharpauni-2 when Matkasur arrived. She got up and headed towards the waterhole. Matkasur followed closely behind. He was clearly in the mood to mate. Maya wasn't interested and kept trying to evade him. But he wouldn't relent. Finally, she lost patience and charged at him with full force. They clashed, sending muddy splashes flying from the waterhole. Their roars echoed through the forest, shaking the surroundings. Within seconds, Matkasur retreated and left the scene. Maya returned to the water—angry and frustrated. She knew this threat hadn't passed, only paused.

Around the same time, Gabbar—Maya's former mate—reappeared in the area. Some of Maya's admirers believe this was her masterstroke. Taking a risk, she ventured out of her territory, found Gabbar and brought him back. They even mated near the Ainbodi waterhole. Eventually, the moment Maya may have

Maya's fierce clash with Matkasur at Pandharpauni-2

desired came true. Matkasur showed up at the Compartment 97 waterhole, where Maya and Gabbar were mating. Both males wanted her, and neither was willing to back down.

They snarled, then lunged at each other—fiercely battling like seasoned wrestlers. Rising on their hind legs, they swiped and clawed at each other with their massive paws, kicking up clouds of dust. Their roars split the air. Matkasur was aggressive, but Gabbar had experience on his side. In the end, Gabbar prevailed. Young Matkasur, bloodied and beaten, retreated towards Jamni Lake, nursing deep gashes on his face and snout.

Maya had finally driven away her biggest threat. But not for too long ...

Surgical Strike

Matkasur soon returned, and this time, Maya could not avoid him. On 3 March 2017, the two were spotted together on Kuhipat road, clear evidence that Maya had finally accepted him. The very next day, Matkasur hunted a sambar and presented it to Maya as a gift. From then on, the two were often seen together.

Usually, a tiger and tigress mate for about a week, but Maya and Matkasur's union lasted much longer. Throughout March and April, they were observed mating, including at the 97 waterhole, the same spot where Matkasur had once lost to Gabbar. It was believed that Matkasur was with Maya when fire watcher Mangaldas Chaudhary got killed on 1 May 2017.

On 8 April 2017, the pair was resting near Tadoba Lake. They hadn't hunted in several days, and both were visibly restless. Matkasur spotted a large wild boar grazing nearby. Using the cover of thick bushes, he crept closer and launched an attack. However, the boar's natural instincts kicked in, and it managed to escape Matkasur's claws. Frustrated, he wandered off in search for easier prey.

As the sun began to set, Maya rose, stretched her limbs and headed towards the lake to quench her thirst. While she was drinking water, a large herd of spotted deer arrived at the lake on the same bank. The herd included several females, young fawns and a majestic stag with sprawling antlers. Acting as the head of his herd, the stag cautiously surveyed the scene and spotted Maya in the distance. Sensing the danger, he stiffened, his tail raised, and stomped his right hoof hard against the ground, letting out a loud 'auw'! The sharp call echoed through the forest, shifting the mood. The entire herd, grazing and drinking water, instantly froze, eyes fixed on Maya. They were all poised

Maya with her trophy after a successful, calculated strike

to flee at any moment.

Tigers usually ignore alarm calls, but not Maya. As soon as the stag cried out, Maya's attention zeroed in on the herd. They were still quite a distance away. She sat still, watching. Another 'auw' rang out. This time, her gaze fixed on the stag. Her expression changed. Without taking her eyes off him, she stood.

A hunt was on her mind. In a heartbeat, she dashed forward like a sprinter from the blocks. Panic ensued and the entire herd scattered in all directions. Maya swiftly charged into the chaos. A fawn came within her reach, but she ignored it. Her focus was entirely on the stag, who was farther than the others. But Maya had targeted the leader who had sounded the alarm. The stag, momentarily confused by this unexpected behaviour, made the fatal mistake Maya had anticipated—he ran towards the water. He didn't get far. Maya closed the gap with terrifying speed, clamped her jaws around his neck and dragged his lifeless body to the shore.

By hunting a big prey, she had ensured enough food for herself and Matkasur.

Rudra Avatar

Maya's anger—a rare glimpse for tourists

30 June 2017. The last day of the tourism season in the core zone. Visitors were eager to soak in as much of the forest's beauty as they could. Scattered showers had fallen since the morning and the gypsy drivers had their hoods up. As always, the vehicles set out on their routes, with tourists hoping for one final sighting—of Maya.

Four vehicles from Moharli Gate eventually reached Ambepat. A vehicle from Kolara Gate soon joined. The guides conferred and decided to wait there for a while. Everyone hoped the season would end with a glimpse of the queen of Tadoba.

Everyone's patience was soon rewarded. Maya made her trademark grand entrance. Like a top batsman sizing up the field, she glanced at the assembled gypsies, seemingly checking whether the cameras were ready to capture her. Then she posed—elegantly, commandingly—in the middle of the road. Shutters clicked furiously. And then—it happened.

A flash accidentally went off. Using a flash photography in the jungle is strictly prohibited, as it disturbs the animals. A photographer had slipped up, and its consequences were swift. Maya's demeanour changed instantly. She shot a furious glance at the vehicles. Moments earlier, she had been calmly indulging her fans—now she was enraged. Her lips curled slightly, creases formed above her nose, her eyes widened and her ears flattened.

Maya's gaze was fixed on the vehicles as if trying to identify who had made the blunder. The experienced guides and drivers quickly realized: Maya was furious! They began reversing quickly. But Maya, now agitated, charged. Fear gripped everyone. She would close in in just a few seconds, and it wouldn't take her long to pull someone out of the vehicle. Some tourists began praying, some screamed, a few even started crying. Who could save them now? God, fate or Maya herself?

The enraged Maya sprinted forward. Just as she was about to leap onto the front vehicle, the people inside squeezed their eyes shut in terror. Chaos erupted. And then, she stopped. She had halted barely a foot away from the vehicle. Everyone stared in disbelief. It was the first time they had witnessed the wrathful side of the queen of Tadoba. Maya stood tall in front of the vehicle, her attack paused mid-charge. The driver didn't dare move the vehicle; even the slightest motion could provoke her further. Her anger still hadn't subsided, and her eyes remained locked on the vehicle. The tension in the air was palpable. The guides, drivers, tourists—all were silent. They could only hear their own heartbeats. Throats were dry. Minds raced with fear. What next? Would Maya attack again?

Maya remained fixed in place. It was as if she was warning them: 'You made a mistake today. Don't repeat it. I won't be so kind next time.'

Once she was satisfied that the offending humans had learned their lesson, Maya turned and walked away without a backward glance. She made her way to a nearby ditch, as if trying to cool both her body and her anger.

What Maya had delivered that day is known as a mock charge. Tigers, contrary to popular perception, are generally gentle creatures. They use such bluff charges to express displeasure or give a warning. A mock charge offers the other party a chance to retreat. Elephants, other wild animals and even venomous snakes often issue similar warnings before launching an actual attack. It is our responsibility to understand these signals.

The experienced guides understood Maya's warning. As soon as she turned her back, the drivers swiftly reversed the vehicles. Everyone breathed a sigh of relief. They had all witnessed an entirely new side of their beloved Maya.

Surya and Meera

IN OCTOBER 2017, MAYA BECAME A MOTHER FOR THE THIRD TIME. This time, she had two cubs—one male and one female. The male was named Surya, the female Meera. Under the protection of their powerful father, Matkasur, and their fierce mother, the cubs began to grow. Photographers were once again thrilled, capturing the playful antics of the young ones.

With Surya and Meera, Maya successfully raised cubs to adulthood for the first time—thanks in part to Matkasur. He proved to be a steady presence, often seen with the cubs and supporting Maya with their protection duties.

When the cubs turned one, a remarkable incident occurred. On the morning of 12 October 2018, Forest Guard Sheetal Kulmethe was patrolling the Tadoba beat with her two assistants.

Surya and Meera, sheltered under the watchful presence of Maya

The siblings on the verge of being separated from their mother

As they approached the Pandharpauni—Kala Amba road, they encountered Maya sitting on the path. Tourist jeeps were parked on the opposite side, their cameras trained on her. When the team arrived, Maya glanced at them once before lying down. Judging the situation wisely, the forest guard decided to retreat. Just as they were about to turn back, Surya and Meera, the sibling cubs, appeared. Upon seeing the three humans standing about 200 metres away, the curious cubs started walking towards them.

In the forest, an encounter with a fully grown tiger is often less risky; as adults tend to avoid humans. But young cubs, driven by curiosity, can be unpredictable. Trying to run in such a situation is inviting death. Sheetal and her assistants knew this. They slowly began to back away, pausing at intervals to contact the office via wireless radio, but their attempts failed. Each time they stopped, so did the cubs. As the forest patrol team backed away, the cubs advanced again. On the other side of the road, the tourist vehicles could do nothing. All three tigers were now on the road, and the rocky terrain made it impossible to manoeuvre around them. The tension was palpable.

Then unexpectedly, the cubs halted and looked back. They seemed to realize they were about to step out of their mother's line of sight. A moment later, they turned around and trotted back to Maya.

The patrol team sighed in relief.

Chota Matka

It was past noon, and the safari hours had long ended. Range Forest Officer (RFO) Manisha Jadhav was patrolling the jungle in her vehicle. This was her first posting in Tadoba after joining the forest department, where she led the Chimur Unit of the Special Tiger Protection Force (STPF). As she neared Tadoba Lake, she saw Maya resting in the shade along the shore. Surya and Meera, then about eight to nine months old, were with her. The cubs, still closely attached to their mother, followed her wherever she went and obeyed her every command. Even now, they sat quietly as their mother rested. The atmosphere around the lake was of utter serenity.

Suddenly, Maya stood up. The tension in her muscles was evident—and it showed on her face. Her eyes fixed on something in the distance, she flicked her tail once in the air. It was a signal. Instantly, both cubs sprang up and bolted away. Obeying their mother's coded command, they vanished in no time. A moment later, Maya ran in the opposite direction. Something had triggered the alarm.

Across the lake, Maya had spotted a tiger walking on the road in the non-tourism area. It was Chota Matka, the son of her mate Matkasur and her neighbour, Choti Tara. Chota Matka had recently separated from his mother and was now wandering in search of his own territory. His quest had brought him into Maya's territory that day, posing a potential threat to her cubs.

Near a sign by the lake that warned visitors against swimming, Maya intercepted him. A confrontation seemed imminent. Although Maya was older, she was smaller in both size and weight than Chota Matka. But her aggression was unmistakable. The force of her presence alone made Chota Matka submit instantly.

Maya in an aggressive stance as Chota Matka surrenders completely

He dropped to the ground and pressed his belly, acknowledging Maya's dominance. Looking pitiful, he accepted defeat without a fight. Maya circled him with deliberate, powerful strides as if warning him: 'Leave my territory.' When he tried to get up once, she growled and shoved him back into the roadside bushes. There she sat before him for a while, her gaze unrelenting. Chota Matka avoided eye contact, burying his head between his large paws. The moment he got a chance, he fled.

Later Chota Matka would rise to become one of Tadoba's most dominant tigers, challenging older males, carrying the scars of battle and even killing mighty rivals like Bajrang and Bramha in combat.

Surya

Surya with his mother

SURYA WAS THE MORE AGGRESSIVE AND DARING OF MAYA'S TWO CUBS. He was beginning to increasingly reflect Matkasur in both temperament and strength.

One day, while Surya and Meera were leisurely resting at Pandharpauni, Surya noticed something rustling in the grass. Acting on instincts honed by his mother, he stealthily moved towards the sound. As soon as he got close, he pounced. Then, with a swift pounce, he emerged proudly from the grass with a mongoose dangling from his jaws—his first independent kill.

When the cubs were around fifteen months old, one morning found the entire family—Maya, Matkasur and the two cubs—relaxing in the water at Pandharpauni-1. Suddenly, Surya spotted

Surya and Meera attempting to surround the gaur

a gaur grazing nearby. The sight of the massive beast awakened his instincts. He stood, then moved stealthily toward the animal. Reaching the edge of the grass, he crouched low, waiting for the gaur to draw nearer.

Meera followed, circling to flank the gaur from the left. But as she approached the grass and got into position, the gaur noticed her and charged. Meera bolted away to save herself. Seeing his sister under attack, Surya lunged at the gaur, which promptly retreated. Surya chased after it just as Maya, realizing the danger to her cubs, leapt out of the water to follow.

While this drama unfolded, Matkasur remained seated in the water, observing calmly. Eventually, he also got up and casually strolled after Maya. The experienced father seemed to sense that the gaur would neither be hunted nor pose a threat to his cubs.

Surya and Meera hadn't yet realized that attacking a gaur could be a life-threatening endeavour for a tiger.

At one and a half years of age, Surya left his mother in search of his own territory. Travelling nearly 70 to 80 kilometres, he reached the Umred–Karhandla Wildlife Sanctuary, where he established a territory and found a companion in a tigress named Fairy.

Meera

After Surya left, Maya injured her left eye—possibly during a fight with an intruding tiger or while hunting. She stayed in the non-tourism area behind Pandharpauni until her injury was fully healed.

By this time, Meera was nearly two years old and still living with her mother. She had started hunting independently. In the first week of October 2019, Meera was spotted near Tadoba Lake. She looked extremely weak and injured, with deep wounds on her neck, stomach and back. Hunting was out of the question; even walking seemed difficult. She stayed in the area for two days but then disappeared. As a result, the forest department launched a search operation.

Meera bearing deep wounds in her final days

Maya retreating into seclusion after injuring her left eye

On the morning of 7 October, around 8.30 a.m., a search team consisting of Forest Guard Sheetal Kulmethe, labourer Nannavare and two other daily-wage workers reached the Panchdhara area near the Tadoba temple. They noticed a foul smell. As they moved closer to an old well surrounded by lantana bushes, they found Meera's lifeless body. Many hours had passed since her death, and maggots had begun to infest her face. One eye protruded from its socket, her right hind paw was torn and flesh was exposed from her lower abdomen. None of her body parts were missing.

Senior forest officials quickly arrived at the scene and conducted a thorough inspection. Meera's body was measured: weight—94.400 kg, length from nose to tail—172 cm, tail length—90 cm, chest girth—110 cm, and height from back to paw—100 cm.

After completing the documentation, Meera's body was brought to the road near the Tadoba colony for a postmortem. Dr P. D. Kadukar, Dr Kundan Padechalwar and Dr Ravikant Khobragade performed the autopsy. It was concluded that Meera had died naturally forty-eight hours earlier due to severe internal injuries and spinal damage resulting from a violent struggle. The postmortem report suggested that the fight likely occurred over territorial disputes, indicating a clash with another tiger. It is widely believed that Meera was injured while hunting a gaur, as some tourists had recently seen her attempting to take one down.

Regardless of the cause, it was a tragic end for a young and daring tigress. After the postmortem, Meera's body was cremated.

The Mystery

Maya's behaviour could sometimes leave everyone puzzled

There was a perplexing incident that occurred shortly after Meera's death.

Until 2020, the forest staff colony was located along the banks of Tadoba Lake. The Tadoba Range Office stood where the 'Visava' interpretation centre now stands. There was no mobile network coverage in the colony, so staff would walk to a spot on the Katezari road behind the colony to make calls. That was the only place with signal reception.

On the morning of 10 October 2019, Dinesh Meshram, a clerk at the Range Office, went to that spot with a labourer to make a call. As Meshram pulled out his phone, he noticed something moving on the ground. When he bent down to inspect it, he was shocked. It was a tiny tiger cub, delicate, no bigger than a palm and newly born! Its umbilical cord was still attached. Overcome with emotion, Meshram immediately called RFO Satish Shende and informed him about the situation. Acting swiftly, Shende ordered the Katezari road closed to the public. Shortly afterward, Shende, Divisional Forest Officer (DFO) Nanasaheb Ladkat and other staff arrived and inspected the cub.

The cub had clearly been born just a few hours earlier, but the mother was nowhere to be seen. She had possibly gone out to drink water or hunting and was expected to return soon. It was decided to keep a distant watch on the cub. A labourer was positioned on a nearby tree to monitor the site, while the rest of the team dispersed.

The big question was: whose cub was this? The site was part of Maya's territory. Beyond it lay the territory of the Katezari female. So, was the cub born to one of them? Or had a new, inexperienced tigress ventured into the area to give birth? Everyone hoped answers would emerge as the day progressed.

From his perch, the labourer maintained a close watch. The morning passed, but the tigress did not appear. As the sun climbed, a tigress approached from a distance along the Katezari road. The mystery of the cub's identity seemed close to resolution. The labourer focused intently—it was the Katezari female. She walked along the road for a while but did not approach the cub. Instead, she turned back and left the way she had come. After that, there was silence again. The cub's mother never appeared, even as the day ended.

Around 8 to 8.30 p.m., the officials met again to reassess the situation. The forest department usually avoids intervening in the natural life cycle of wildlife. It was decided to wait through the night and, if the tigress did not return by morning, to take the cub into custody and try to save it. Since no one could monitor the site overnight, a camera trap was set up at the site.

The next morning, when the team returned, they noticed

male tiger tracks in the soil. Their hearts sank. It wasn't the tigress who had visited during the night but a male tiger. As they moved further, their worst fear was confirmed. They found half-eaten remains of the tiny cub. Deeply saddened, they checked the camera trap hoping to identify the tiger responsible. But the camera had been knocked over, likely by the tiger itself. No images had been recorded. The mystery of who had killed the cub remained unsolved.

But whose cub was it?

RFO Shende had figured out the answer the previous day. After posting the labourer in the tree to monitor the cub, he had gone on patrol. Near the staff quarters, he saw Maya by the lakeside guest house. She was bleeding from her rear. That confirmed it—the cub was hers.

But then, why had she abandoned her newborn? Why hadn't she returned, either during the day or night? No one ever found answers to these questions.

Rudra and Tala

In 2018, two male tigers from the Kolsa range—Rudra and Tala, brothers—entered Maya's territory. Like Matkasur before them, they mated with Maya. Among them, Tala was exceptionally strong. He challenged Matkasur and the fierce battle between the two resulted in Tala emerging victorious. During this time, Chota Matka, the young son of Matkasur and Choti Tara, was still searching for his own territory, but he too was driven away by the brothers. Eventually, a fight broke out between the two brothers,

The mating pair—Tala and Maya

Rudra and Maya

and Tala emerged as the dominant one.

Tala now reigned over Maya's stronghold—Pandharpauni. He became a familiar sight, often seen cooling off in the water. One scorching afternoon, when I arrived at Pandharpauni-1, Tala was resting in the water. Just then, a large sambar deer approached. The sambar was startled at seeing the tiger in the water, but it was too thirsty to flee. Tala showed no interest. He glanced at the deer once and remained still. The sambar drank quickly and left.

Though Tala reigned over Pandharpauni, Rudra and Matkasur never entirely left Maya's territory. They kept their distance from Tala, but were occasionally spotted.

The Strategist

Maya, in many ways, was like any other tigress. But her behaviour often revealed a level of strategy that set her apart. Unlike most tigers who rely purely on instinct, Maya's actions frequently seemed deliberate—as if she weighed her options before making a move.

An incident in January 2020 highlighted this quality once again.

That day, tourist vehicles had parked near the Pandharpauni area hoping to catch a glimpse of her. Soon, alarm calls from spotted deer and monkeys signalled her arrival. As expected, Maya emerged onto the road and began walking in front of the vehicles. Tourists were thrilled, thinking they would get plenty of time to observe and photograph her. But within minutes, she slipped into the tall grass near the Pandharpauni-2 waterhole, leaving them disappointed. While some vehicles left, others decided to wait. Those who had seen Maya in action before knew better—she was full of surprises. Their patience would be duly rewarded.

As she walked along, Maya had spotted something near the waterhole. She left the road and disappeared into the grass. Attentive tourists could see her moving stealthily towards the waterhole. Only the arch of her back was visible as she crept forward. Her taut body language left no doubt—she was preparing for a hunt. But what was her target?

At the waterhole, a female sambar deer was drinking water with her fawn. Maya had spotted them and was now closing in. To catch them off guard, she positioned herself behind the pair, hiding in the grass. Her movements were slow and calculated, every step placed with precision. Tourists watched the scene

Maya hunting a sambar fawn

breathlessly. An attack seemed imminent. However, before she could pounce, the sambar sensed danger and began scanning its surroundings. Realizing she couldn't wait any longer, Maya charged at the sambar. Startled, the mother fled. After some distance, she looked back only to realize Maya's true plan. It was too late. The attack had been a ruse. Maya's real intention was to separate the mother from her fawn, and she succeeded. As the adult deer ran, Maya turned her attention towards the fawn. In its panic, the fawn ran towards the water, sealing its fate. Maya caught it with a single leap.

Lockdown-1

In 2020, the Covid-19 pandemic brought the world to a standstill. The Government of India announced a nationwide lockdown. From 18 March, all tourism activities in reserve came to a halt. However, the rhythms of all wildlife, including Maya, continued as usual. Maya was pregnant. By the end of the month, she stopped appearing before forest officials, raising concerns. Had she given birth? Was she safe? Finally, it was decided to launch a search operation.

On the morning of 11 April, two teams set out to search within Maya's territory. One team headed towards Pandharpauni and spotted her there. Her stomach was visibly flattened, confirming she had delivered her fourth litter. Everyone was relieved to find her safe. But where were the cubs, and were they safe?

The second team of six moved towards Ainbodi, led by Forest Guard Sheetal Kulmethe of the Tadoba beat. At 8.57 a.m., at the rear of Ainbodi near the Waghai stream they discovered a litter of cubs huddled in a rocky crevice—five in total. The cubs were

The newborn cubs nestled in a rocky crevice near the Waghai stream—Maya's fourth litter

so young their eyes hadn't yet opened. It was the first time Maya had given birth to five cubs. The team was overjoyed and quickly returned to share the news. It wasn't until June that Maya's fans got wind of the happy development, when newspapers published the story, bringing much-needed cheer during the lockdown.

The following day, Sheetal and her team returned to the stream—only to find the cubs gone. Maya seemed to have moved them overnight, likely after sensing human presence. Even more surprising was that after they had left the area the previous day, Maya had walked the same path the team had taken. Her pugmarks were imprinted in the soil. Had she tracked the scent of individuals who had been near her cubs? Perhaps. The protective mother had realized the location was no longer safe for her cubs.

That same afternoon, around 4 p.m., Maya and Matkasur were spotted together at Ainbodi. Since Tala had fathered the cubs, Maya was now trying to keep Matkasur away from them.

Three days later, Sheetal had another unforgettable encounter. While on foot patrol with a team of ten, they reached the dry stream behind Pandharpauni-2. To cross it, they had to climb a small embankment. Eager to reach the top quickly, Sheetal sprinted up the slope. When she got there, her heart skipped a beat. Maya was sitting right in front. The tigress was so close, she could have attacked in an instant. Neither Sheetal nor her team had realized Maya was there. But Maya had been observing them since they descended into the stream. Even with Sheetal standing so close, Maya remained calm. She simply glanced at Sheetal before shifting her gaze to the labourers walking in the stream below. Seizing the moment, Sheetal quietly retreated. She alerted her colleagues and led them safely away.

On 1 October 2020, tourism resumed in the core area, and visitors returned to the reserve. This time, Maya and her four cubs were seen thriving in the Pandharpauni area. One of the cubs had died during this period, though the circumstances of its death remain unknown.

Cubs Missing?

Maya with her four cubs at Pandharpauni

Around two and a half months after Maya gave birth, some newspapers ran sensational headlines: 'All of Maya's Cubs are Dead!' Several articles suggested that only one cub had died, while three were still alive. During this time, tourism was shut again due to the lockdown. These stories, based on unnamed sources, gained traction. It was true that the forest staff hadn't seen the cubs for ten to fifteen days, but the media had jumped to conclusions. This prompted senior officials to launch a search operation led by Kolara RFO Pradeep Chavan.

The Kolara Range had just been newly established, carved out from the Tadoba Range. Both the Pandharpauni waterholes fell under Kolara. Chavan was the first RFO of this new range. Fresh from training, this was his first posting. This search mission was his first significant fieldwork. He led a team of twenty to twenty-two people, including the Kolara staff, forest workers and personnel from the Chimur STPF, to locate Maya's cubs.

The plan was to search on foot in areas inaccessible by vehicles. Behind the Pandharpauni waterholes, in the non-tourism zone, lies the Mahapinki stream. The team cautiously descended into the dry stream bed and began their search. Despite careful effort, they found no signs of the cubs. After some time, the team took a break and sat down in the stream bed. Minutes later, they resumed the search.

A young member of the team, Mangesh, was leading the way. As they rounded a bend in the stream, he suddenly turned and whispered, 'Maya is sitting there.' Unexpectedly, he had come very close to her, but Maya showed no signs of aggression. Once they realized she was blocking the path, RFO Chavan decided not to proceed further. The team slowly retreated about 50 metres to a corner from where they could clearly see her. She appeared relaxed and unbothered. But she wasn't alone—her cubs were playing nearby!

The team was relieved to see them. However, they noticed there were only three cubs. Where was the fourth? RFO Chavan set up camera traps in the area to monitor further, and the team withdrew.

Back in the vehicle, Chavan decided to check the stream from the opposite side. About half an hour later, they returned from the other side. Maya was still there, but this time all four cubs were present. It seemed that the fourth cub had hidden itself when the search team had approached earlier and came out to play only when it felt safe again.

The timid nature of this cub would later prove to be an asset.

The team was overjoyed to see all four cubs safe and spent a few minutes watching them play. However, Maya kept a watchful eye on their every move. After a while, she let out a low growl, signalling her displeasure. RFO Chavan immediately instructed everyone to leave the area.

Five days later, the camera traps were checked. They had captured images of all four cubs.

Family Lunch

THIS INCIDENT TOOK PLACE WHEN MAYA'S CUBS WERE AROUND NINE MONTHS OLD. It was around 1.30 in the afternoon. Maya was resting in the shade near Pandharpauni-2, while her cubs were nowhere in sight. She had hidden them somewhere safe.

Suddenly, Maya woke up from her deep sleep. Her posture was alert and cautious. For a few seconds, she stared in the direction of Bamangao, one of the local villages inside the reserve, beyond the waterhole. Then, she slowly moved towards the water, using the island at the centre as cover. In an instant, her relaxed demeanour gave way to that of a predator. She had spotted a family of sambar deer approaching the water. The family consisted of a male, a female and a grown-up fawn. Unaware

Maya communicating with her cubs by just wagging her tail

A mother fulfilling her responsibility by hunting for her family

of Maya's presence, they began drinking water peacefully. In a flash, Maya pounced and took down the fawn.

After securing her kill, she carried it to the island. Would she eat it herself or call her cubs to feed on the tender meat? But she did neither. She carefully hid the prey beneath the grass under a jamun tree, then leisurely stepped into the water. For some time, she swam alone, seemingly enjoying the moment. After a while, she lifted her tail and gave it a slight wag. Immediately, the four cubs, who had been waiting in the bushes near the bank, rushed towards her. The moment they entered the water, they began to splash around and play joyfully while Maya watched with pride.

After a good round of play, Maya made a distinct sound, prompting the cubs to follow her out of the water one by one. Like a mother drying her drenched child's hair, she lovingly groomed and licked them dry. All the play had made them hungry, so she led them back to the island, where she uncovered the hidden kill. Then, they enjoyed a family lunch together under the shade of the jamun tree.

The Third Casualty

After the first Covid lockdown, restrictions eased across the country, and tourism resumed. Meanwhile, the forest department staff continued their routine duties. On 16 December 2020, the fire line clearing began in compartments 71 to 49 in the Chikhlwahi area. Thirty-two labourers—twenty-eight women and four men—from the nearby village of Bamangao were hired for this task. The first day passed without incident. The next day, they reported back to work at 6 a.m. Forest Guard G.M. Japghare instructed them to resume from where they had left off.

At around 8.15 a.m., the workers were divided into three groups. While Japghare was instructing the third group, loud screams suddenly erupted from the first. Sensing that something was wrong, Japghare and others rushed over—barely 15 metres away—and froze at the sight. A tigress had seized a woman by the neck and stood holding her in its jaws. It was clear that the unfortunate woman had no chance of survival. Despite everyone shouting and banging sticks, the tigress began dragging the body away. Hearing the commotion, labourers working nearby in Navegaon meadows rushed to the scene. By then, the tigress had pulled the body 150 metres deep into the paper flower thickets. When everyone reached there, the tigress was standing near the body. Only after repeated shouting did she back off, leaving the body.

Once the tigress was far enough, the workers hurried to retrieve the body. The victim was identified as Vidya Sanjay Waghade, aged forty-two. Her eyes and mouth were slightly open. There were wounds measuring one to one and a half inch in length and about two inches deep on both sides of her neck. Her back had deep claw gashes, from which blood continued to ooze.

Her clothes were soaked in blood, as was the dry grass beneath her. Pugmarks left by the tigress were visible near the body.

Meanwhile, senior forest department officials, police personnel and members of Vidya Waghade's family were informed about the incident. Upon their arrival, a spot inspection was conducted, and the body was sent to the Chimur sub-district hospital for a postmortem. That evening, her last rites were performed in Bamangao amid a sombre atmosphere. The forest department provided the wood for the funeral and extended ₹15 lakh as financial assistance to the victim's family.

Identifying the tigress responsible for the attack posed no difficulty—it was Maya. This was the third human casualty attributed to her.

Why did this happen?

The spot inspection report, i.e. the panchnama, revealed the answer. Maya had been crouching in a low-lying area near the fire line—not to attack humans, but to ambush a herd of spotted deer grazing nearby. She was closely observing the herd, waiting for the right moment to strike. When the opportunity arose, she launched an attack. The herd scattered in panic. Some of them ran towards the fire line, and Maya chased them. Unfortunately, Vidya Waghade, who was seated at the time, was caught between the fleeing deer and the charging tigress, resulting in her tragic death.

A similar incident had occurred in December 2019. On that occasion, a fire line clearing was underway near the lake round. Maya came walking along the tar road leading from the rest house atop the hill. There had been no alarm calls, so no one noticed her approaching. She got as close as five feet from the workers before they realized and froze in fear. However, she did not attack anyone. The labourers slowly backed away and safely retreated to their vehicle. Maya had then calmly moved away.

An illustration of the alleged scene of the incident

Queen of Taru

In January 2021, Maya added another feather to her cap when National Geographic channel released a documentary on her life titled *Tiger Queen of Taru*. The 44-minute film traced her journey—from her early years and her struggles, to raising her cubs, her mates, and the vast territory she ruled. By now Maya was already world-famous, this was the her story was broadcast on a global platform; the film was later dubbed into several languages across the world.

Aishwarya Sridhar, a young filmmaker from Panvel in the Raigad district, had directed this documentary. She had combined footage personally shot by her with scenes captured by other tourists up until 2018. For Maya's fans, watching her on television was a true delight.

When I asked how Maya appeared through her lens, she said, 'Maya may seem like any other tiger, but her story is unique. An orphaned tigress not only survives alone in the jungle but builds an enormous empire and maintains it for over a decade. She strives to make her cubs as strong and independent as herself. To protect them, she mates with multiple males at the same time. Despite being under immense stress, she still manages to charm tourists and photographers. It is beyond imagination.

'Spending time with Maya while shooting made me realize that wild animals also have emotions. When Maya lovingly groomed her cubs, she embodied motherly affection. After her cubs successfully hunted, she would rub against them in appreciation. Watching her wander in a mournful state after losing her cubs was heartbreaking. I saw all the human emotions reflected in her.'

When asked which of Maya's traits had impressed her

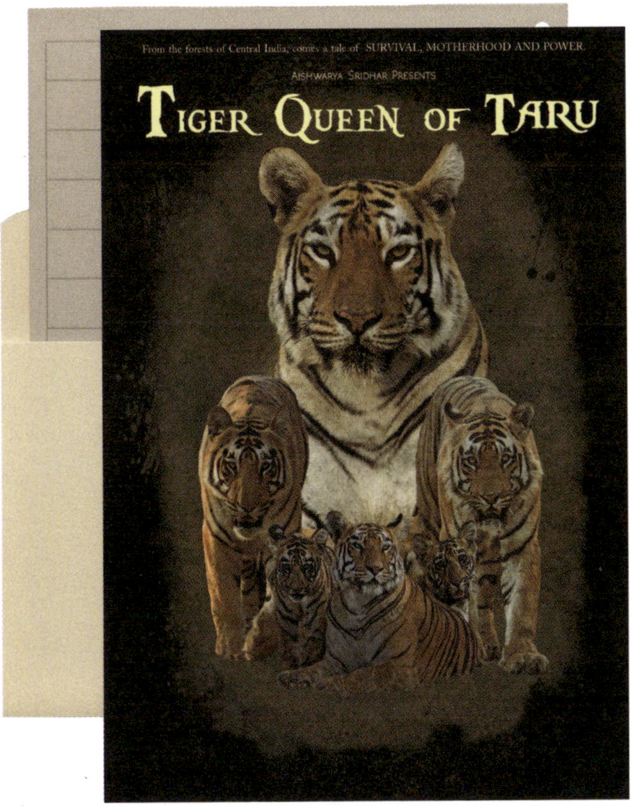

Maya's international screen debut in *Tiger Queen of Taru* (2021)

the most, Aishwarya replied, 'Maya was undoubtedly bold, aggressive, and beautiful. But more importantly, she was incredibly strategic and intelligent. Whether it was bringing back Gabbar to fend off Matkasur or mating with multiple males for the safety of her cubs, she always seemed to think out of the box. Moreover, despite having a large territory, she rarely engaged in battles. Instead of brute strength, she often relied on smart strategies.'

Second Lockdown

The queen in her capital, Pandharpauni

Just when it seemed the threat of the pandemic had subsided, it resurged, prompting another state-imposed lockdown. Tourism in Tadoba was once again suspended, beginning 15 April 2021. During this period, I spent thirty-seven days in Tadoba. My emotional investment in Maya and Tadoba, built over a decade, only deepened during those weeks.

The Tadoba administration had decided to initiate an evaluation process for guides—through both written and oral exams. The results would determine their grading and, consequently, their pay. I was part of the committee responsible for the oral exams.

On the evening of 29 April 2021, after concluding the guide exams at Madanapur, we were on our way back to Moharli through the forest. On a whim, we decided to take a detour to Pandharpauni-2. The scene there seemed calm. Two peafowls pecked at the waterhole's edge, and a sambar stood knee-deep in the water. Our driver remarked, 'Since everything is so peaceful, Maya must not be here. Let's move on.' He began to turn the vehicle around.

I was sitting in the back seat, looking at the waterhole through the rear window. Suddenly, I shouted, 'Tiger!, Tiger!', having spotted a figure on the slope of the island in the waterhole. I could make out from its posture it was a tiger. When the driver reversed, everyone saw what I had spotted: a young tiger, around a year old, sitting gracefully on the slope, observing the sambar calmly. It was one of Maya's cubs.

We moved the vehicle to the other side of the waterhole for a better view. The cub had now got up and retreated into the grass on the island. Moments later, another cub emerged from behind a rock right in front of our vehicle and walked along the edge. The first cub also returned and followed. Together, they climbed the embankment, then disappeared into the tall grass.

Just then, one of my colleagues exclaimed, 'Maya!' We looked up. There she was—sitting beneath a tree on the embankment where the cubs had gone. She was right in front of us, looking

A tiger hunts only when hungry

every bit a queen seated on her throne. She had probably been observing us all along as we watched her cubs, now one year old. The other two cubs were likely hidden in the grass nearby. One of them was known to be so timid that even at that age, it preferred staying close to its mother. It was the same cub that had tried to hide from the search team led by RFO Pradeep Chavan.

You may have realized how the cubs born to the same mother can differ greatly in terms of nature. These differences can be seen from their behaviour at a very young age, and their future in the wild, when they grow up, is shaped mainly by their nature.

I was so engrossed in observing the cubs and Maya, that I hadn't even noticed when the sambar in the water had slipped away. I wondered: how had the sambar, with five tigers around, remained so calm and safe?

Tigers use their energy judiciously. They don't hunt unless hungry and, even then, they hunt only to fill their own and their cubs' bellies. Unlike humans, tigers don't store food. That's why, even in the presence of five tigers, the sambar had managed to come to the water, quench their thirst and leave unscathed.

The Playfight

It was an evening in May 2021. Maya, her mate Tala and their four cubs were resting at Pandharpauni-2. The cubs, then around thirteen to fourteen months old, were growing up fast. It was around 6, and darkness was about to set in. Suddenly, one cub leapt up. Soon, two others followed, their eyes locked in on something moving in the grass. The fourth cub remained still, showing no interest in their adventure.

A full-grown male gaur was grazing in the tall grass. Despite its massive size and bulging muscles that exuded strength, the

Maya's adventurous cubs wished to hunt a gaur

three adventurous cubs had decided to hunt it. Their combined size and weight were insignificant compared to the gaur, but their youthful confidence was high. The trio split up: two positioned themselves in front, while the third circled behind the gaur.

They formed a rough strategy. When the two in front would make a move, the gaur charged at them. Seizing this moment, the third cub would attack from behind. Then, as the gaur turned to face its attacker in the rear, the two cubs in front leapt towards him. This game of bluff and charge continued until nightfall.

Throughout this commotion, Maya occasionally opened her eyes to observe he spectacle but quickly returned to sleep. She seemed content knowing her cubs were safe and didn't interfere. Tala didn't even bother to look. There were six tigers present there that day. Together, they could have easily hunted the gaur. Maya and Tala together, or Tala alone, could have taken it down. But the parents were in no mood for hunting. It was a day of ease for them.

The next morning, the same gaur was seen peacefully grazing nearby, unharmed.

When tourism resumed in June that year, visitors were surprised to find Maya alone. Her cubs were nowhere to be seen. A few days earlier, a male tiger named Mowgli had been spotted at Pandharpauni-2. Many assumed he had killed all of Maya's cubs, as no remains were found. However, one cub had survived—the shyest of the litter, who was always hiding. His timid nature had saved his life. He would occasionally be spotted but would quickly flee upon seeing vehicles.

One night, around 8 p.m., as I was travelling through the forest after work, I spotted him in the glow of the headlights. By then, he had grown into a fully mature adult male. Yet his nature hadn't changed. On seeing the vehicle, he started bounding down the road, startled. Watching a tiger in his prime—especially Maya's cub—fleeing nervously like this was astonishing.

He was only the second of Maya's cubs after Surya to survive. In time he was named 'Y Mark' for a unique Y-shaped stripe pattern on his body. Others called him 'Sanju'. Eventually, he moved to the Lohara buffer zone, from where he sometimes wandered into the Moharli buffer area.

The STPF

In August 2021, Forest Guard Piyushkumar Chakre joined the Special Tiger Protection Force (STPF), an elite force tasked with protecting the forest against poaching and deforestation. STPF patrols run day and night. They inspect trails for traps set by poachers, check waterholes for poison and ensure the tiger kills near villages are not poisoned. Their work becomes especially challenging during the monsoon, when dense grass, tangled bushes and flooded swamps make every step difficult and dangerous. At times they must wade through chest-deep water, not knowing when a wild animal might cross their path. Armed only with a stick for defence, their patrols continue uninterrupted.

In such conditions, Chakre set out on his first patrol alongside eleven colleagues. Entering the forest through the Kolara gate at 6 a.m., they drove a few kilometres, then disembarked and proceeded on foot. The damp monsoon air had a pleasant coolness, and the earthy aroma soothed the senses. Around them the landscape was lush with varying shades of green, the red-dirt path meandering through the jungle vividly.

The team advanced cautiously on the Kolara–Pandharpauni trail, with Chakre and a colleague leading, and the rest following at a distance. Unbeknownst to them, the gap between the front and rear groups had widened. When Chakre and his companion reached the trail's intersection, sweat began to bead on their foreheads despite the cool weather. Standing right in front of them was Maya.

While the STPF members were walking one path, Maya was approaching from another in the same direction. They had unexpectedly come face-to-face at the junction. As Maya

The STPF personnel often encountered Maya

stopped in her tracks, the situation became critical for Chakre and his colleague. Their fellow guards, unaware of the situation, were still far behind. At that moment, the two men were alone, facing Maya. It was a precarious situation where a single mistake could prove fatal.

At that critical moment, they recalled the training they had received. It was the time to show their presence of mind. They raised their sticks high, trying to appear as large as possible. Also, they began shouting loudly to deter Maya from coming closer. Hearing their cries, the rest of the team rushed to their aid. The senior members quickly instructed, 'Don't panic. Stay together. Don't try to run.' All twelve members stood together, raised their sticks and continued to shout loudly.

Maya, however, remained unfazed. She stood calmly in the middle of the path, observing the commotion. At one point, she lifted her front paw, sending a chill down Chakre's spine. Fear gripped everyone. Was she about to charge? How would they defend themselves? Their minds raced with panic.

But Maya had a different plan. She slowly lowered her paw, gazed at them for some time, then turned and disappeared into the bushes. Relief washed over the team as they embraced each other and thanked God.

However, not everyone was as lucky as they were.

The Fourth Casualty

20 November 2021. It was 6 in the morning. A small team gathered at the Kolara Protection Hut. Forest Guard Swati Dhumane briefed her team, which included three forest labourers: Nikhil Bagde, Ashok Nagose and Rakesh Nannaware. She ensured the range finder and GPS device were working properly. Everyone grabbed their sticks, took a quick group photo outside the hut and set off precisely at 6.45 a.m.

The team was carrying out a transect line survey—an annual exercise conducted across all forest ranges. The data collected from this survey helps estimate the population of both herbivores and carnivores. Swati's team was assigned to survey the carnivores. The task required them to walk in a straight line for five kilometres, documenting any carnivores sightings or signs of their presence, such as calls, scat or tracks. The assignment demanded their utmost alertness.

At the same time, several other groups were conducting similar surveys throughout the reserve.

Swati's team was walking along the boundary of compartments 96 and 97, recording their observations. It was prime safari time for tourists, but this team was moving through a non-tourism zone, where tourist vehicles were not allowed.

By 7.40 a.m., the team had covered 4.5 kilometres. Just half a kilometre remained to complete their task. Suddenly, they stopped in their tracks. Right in the middle of the road sat Maya—just 200 meters ahead—relaxing in her characteristic regal pose. She was facing the team, clearly aware of their presence but appeared unbothered. Maya was sitting on the boundary of the tourism zone. On the opposite side, visitors in safari vehicles were watching and photographing her. It made for a striking

An imagined rendering of the incident scene

scene—the forest staff looking at Maya, Maya sitting serenely on the road, surrounded by golden grass and green trees.

Swati and her team waited for some time, hoping Maya would move off the path so they could continue their work. However, Maya showed no intention of leaving. After about 16 minutes of waiting, Swati made a critical decision: they would bypass Maya by taking a detour. Accordingly, all four of them turned left and entered the dense bamboo forest. Walking through the bamboo thicket, they continued towards 97 waterhole. Nikhil was leading, and Swati was walking at the rear. Low-hanging bamboos forced them to crouch as they walked. Over the next 8 to 10 minutes, they had covered around 200 metres.

Then Nikhil suddenly heard a sound. He crouched and scanned the area. His heart skipped a beat when he spotted the familiar striped pattern in the bamboo. Ashok, walking just behind him, also sensed the danger. Both shouted, 'Tiger! Tiger!' But before they could fully utter the words, Maya had already pounced on Swati, the last in line, sinking her canines into her neck. The terrified labourers screamed, but it did not affect Maya. She dragged Swati back towards the road.

The three labourers ran towards the path leading to the waterhole. They tried to communicate via wireless, but the dense forest made it impossible. Desperate, they rushed to the tourist vehicles for help. The tourists, guides and gypsy drivers had heard the screams but hadn't seen what had happened. The labourers were then driven to Kolara Protection Hut, where they sent out a wireless message at 8.20 a.m.: 'Forest Guard Swati Dhumane has been attacked and dragged away by a tiger!'

At that moment, deputy director of the Core Zone Nandkishor Kale was inspecting the survey in the Teliya area of the Moharli range. Upon hearing the distressed message, he immediately headed towards Kolara. Round Officer Lonare, working at Jamni Chowk, also rushed to the Kolara Kuti first and then to the scene with the three labourers. Upon investigating, they found drag marks leading away from the attack site.

By 8.40 a.m., Deputy Director Kale's vehicle reached the spot. A search operation began under his guidance. With the possibility of the tigress being nearby, everyone was instructed to make loud noises as they moved. They started their search, following the drag marks. At some distance, the team first found Swati's GPS device. Then, one after another, they found other items—a range finder, diary and pen. They also discovered a blood-stained black scarf and eventually reached the road where Maya had initially been sitting. She had dragged Swati across the road. The search team crossed it and found Swati's mobile phone. Further along, they collected pieces of her blood-soaked clothing. The trail led them to Jambulpat Nallah, where the water was stained red with blood. Fresh tiger pugmarks were clearly visible in the mud along the bank.

The search team cautiously crossed the stream and moved ahead. It was now close to 9 a.m. After covering about 150 metres, they encountered a heart-wrenching sight. Blood was splattered everywhere. Swati's lifeless body lay amidst the bamboo, her head severed from the torso. The left side of her chest was mauled up to the shoulder. The postmortem later revealed a total of eight deep wounds on her skull.

The incident cast a pall of grief over the entire forest department. Swati Dhumane's family was provided a financial assistance of ₹15 lakh, along with additional support from donations. Her husband was also offered a job in the forest department. The transect line survey was immediately suspended. Staff unions demanded that future surveys be conducted only with adequate protection. The news received widespread media coverage.

A part of Maya's territory was temporarily closed to tourists. The tigress, once known for brushing against tourist vehicles, was now being treated with caution. Gypsy drivers were instructed to maintain a minimum distance of 50 metres from her.

What Went Wrong?

After the unfortunate death of Forest Guard Swati Dhumane, the inevitable question arose: what exactly had gone wrong? Two days after the incident, I reached Tadoba and was able to gather further insight into the situation.

The most critical detail lies in the working protocols of the forest department: if any danger is sensed while working in the jungle, the concerned personnel must immediately retreat to a safe shelter, abandoning the task at hand. In this case, the threat was visible in the form of a tigress sitting on the road.

The second—perhaps more consequential—decision was to leave the road and cut through the forest. On the road, they were at a safe distance of around 200 metres from Maya. But inside the dense forest, that distance came down to just 100

Maya, moments before the tragic encounter with Swati Dhumane's team

metres or so. It brought them directly into her line of sight.

Crouching low while they moved through the bamboo thickets, their silhouettes may have resembled potential prey—a deer or a sambar. Following her instincts, she began to stalk them and launch an attack.

Considering the sequence of events, it is difficult to blame Maya for this tragic incident. Wild predators tend to follow their natural instincts when faced with what they perceive as a threat. Still, this incident once again raised questions about Maya's behaviour. Was it too dangerous to work on foot in her territory? Would she now prevent patrols, surveys or other human activities in her area? Had her attitude towards humans changed? Was she no longer the Maya we once knew? Such questions troubled her fans.

In truth, these concerns were largely baseless. Forest staff had worked in her territory before and continued to do so after the incident. Many encountered her. None were attacked.

In the days that followed, biologist Prajakta Hushangabadkar closely monitored Maya to observe any changes in her behaviour. I accompanied her on these outings a few times as well. To us, she seemed unchanged. Once, Prajakta stopped our vehicle about 50 metres from Maya and got down cautiously to see her reaction, leaving the car door open for a quick retreat if needed. Maya just sat there calmly, without showing any signs of aggression.

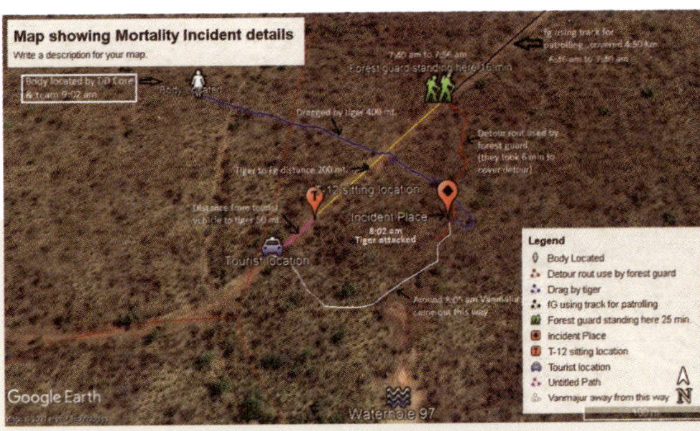

A map depicting the events leading to the forest guard's tragic death

The Fortunate One

ANOTHER INCIDENT OCCURRED JUST TWO DAYS BEFORE THE TRAGIC DEATH OF SWATI DHUMANE—ON THE EVENING OF NOVEMBER 18, 2021. Around 5.30 p.m., Divisional Forest Officer (DFO) Shatanik Bhagwat was returning from a day of work, heading from Tadoba to Jamunbodi in a department vehicle with his driver. As they approached 97 waterhole, a few tourist vehicles approached from the opposite direction. To make way, the driver edged the slightly vehicle off the road. But the dew-wet grass betrayed them and the wheels slipped and slid into a roadside ditch. The vehicle was tilted dangerously. Any attempt to accelerate could have tipped it over.

They cautiously exited the vehicle and tried unsuccessfully to relay a message to the office via wireless. They could have requested help from the tourist vehicles, but DFO Bhagwat, known for his discipline, was reluctant to inconvenience tourists who had paid for their safari experience. He decided to walk a short distance to seek help. He knew full well the risk—they would traverse Maya's territory—a risky endeavour. But with nightfall approaching, they had no choice but to act quickly.

DFO Bhagwat thought heading towards Tadoba Lake would be more dangerous, so they opted to walk towards Kolara road to seek help. The two men began walking briskly yet cautiously, silently praying nothing untoward would happen. The tension was so intense they lost track of both time and distance. Eventually, when they reached Jamni Chowk, they spotted a forest department vehicle approaching. They hitched a ride back to the spot where their vehicle was stuck, realizing along the way they had walked approximately 4.5 to 5 kilometres through Maya's territory!

The stranded vehicle was then successfully pulled out with the help of the arriving team.

The relief was short-lived. A day after this incident, Swati Dhumane was fatally attacked by Maya. When the news of her death reached DFO Bhagwat, he was deeply shaken. The full weight of the near-miss struck him: what had spared them that evening was sheer luck.

Although Maya was affectionate, she was still a wild tiger in her natural habitat

A Miracle

Four days after Forest Guard Swati Dhumane's death, Biologist Prajakta, GIS (Geographic Information System) expert Shahebaj Sheikh and I went into the forest to observe Maya's state of mind. Around 8 or 8.30 in the morning, we spotted her from our vehicle sitting calmly on the Kuhipat road. She appeared peaceful, basking in the morning sun right in the middle of the road. After a while, she got up and disappeared into the bushes. We moved on.

Just then, we saw a tourist jeep approaching. Guide Sanjay Mankar stood up and signalled us to stop. A seasoned guide in Tadoba, Sanjay had met us earlier that day, and knew we were on the Kuhipat road. But now, he and the tourists in his jeep looked visibly tense. As soon as we drew near, Sanjay called out, 'I found a woman!'

A woman—in the jungle? We were surprised. Sure enough, a woman dressed in a traditional nine-yard sari was in the jeep with the tourists.

Prajakta asked, 'Where did you find her?'

'She was walking along the Pandharpauni road. I picked her up and was on my way to you,' Sanjay replied.

We thanked Sanjay and the tourists for their quick thinking. Taking the woman into our vehicle, we informed deputy director of the Core Zone, Nandkishor Kale, and Kolara RFO Pradeep Chavan. Then we headed to the Kolara Range Office.

On the way, we tried to speak with her. It became clear her mental state was unstable. She couldn't coherently tell us her name, village or anything about her family. Her dialect didn't seem local to Vidarbha. The only details she mentioned a goddess temple in Vani and that she had been deceived by children. She

Maya was friendly, but surviving a night on foot in her territory was nothing short of a miracle

was wearing mismatched slippers and carried a steel plate, bowl and cup in a cloth bag. She was also unable to explain how or when she had entered the forest, or what she was doing there. It seemed she had spent the previous night in the forest but she showed no signs of fear. It was as if she wasn't even aware of the danger the jungle posed.

At the Kolara Range Office, RFO Chavan received her kindly and offered her tea and a meal. He inquired about her situation but we couldn't get much new information. Eventually, it was decided to hand her over to the police, who could trace her family.

Later, Shahebaj used his GIS expertise to create a map of the area. The nearest highway from where the woman had been found was at least 8 kilometres away, making it likely she had indeed spent at least one night in the jungle. In that situation, she could have encountered not just a tiger but also a leopard, sloth bear, wild gaur, or any number of wild animals. Yet she had emerged unharmed.

The most astonishing detail was that Sanjay found her near Pandharpauni—right in Maya's stronghold. Just four days earlier, Maya had killed a female forest guard. Against that backdrop, the fact that this woman survived unscathed could only be described as a miracle.

The last we heard, the police had placed her in a government women's shelter.

Seven Seconds

Maya's reactions were always hard to predict

After the tragic death of Forest Guard Swati Dhumane, safari guides, and drivers were instructed to maintain a safe distance from Maya. The same Maya who once strolled alongside tourist vehicles now had to be observed from afar. In one incident I witnessed myself, tourists in a jeep got so scared upon seeing her that they begged the guide to drive away. Times had changed.

In February 2022, veteran guide Anil Tiwade was on a safari with a group of tourists. Unfortunately for him, they were far more interested in a picnic than the jungle or wildlife. Oblivious to the surrounding birds, trees or the nature, all they kept chanting was, 'Show us the tiger!' Tiwade tried to explain that spotting a tiger is a matter of luck and that the forest had so much more to offer. But they weren't willing to listen.

While this back-and-forth was ongoing, the vehicle headed towards 97 waterhole. The road leading there is narrow and winding, flanked by bamboo clusters on both sides, making it difficult to see what lies ahead. As the jeep rounded a bend, the driver suddenly slammed on the brakes—Maya was sitting in the middle of the road!

Seeing her up close, the chatter of the tourists stopped immediately. Maya, too was startled by the sudden arrival of the vehicle. Theirs was the only vehicle on the road. Maya's body language began to change rapidly—ears flattening, tail twitching in agitation. Tiwade, with years of experience, understood what these signs meant. He instructed the driver keep the engine running and told the tourists to stay quiet and crouch down.

By then, Maya had started sprinting towards the jeep. Tiwade urged everyone to remain still and calm. In a split second, Maya reached the vehicle and reared up, placing her front paws on the bonnet.

The tourists were frozen with fear. The driver, relatively new, was equally terrified. Even Tiwade, who had known Maya since her cubhood, had never seen her in such a menacing form. But he knew staying still was their best strategy. He remained calm and continued to whisper reassurances. Those seven seconds felt endless. Maya stood with her paws on the bonnet, staring at them with piercing eyes. No one dared meet her gaze.

Finally, she lowered her paws, cast a fiery glance at everyone, then turned to walk towards the waterhole. Tiwade instructed the driver to reverse the vehicle slowly. Even after leaving the jungle, the tourists couldn't stop trembling.

Five Males

By the time Maya neared twelve years of age, her territory was contested by five male tigers—Rudra, Tala, Balaram, Mowgli and Yuvraj. She was observed mating with all of them. This naturally placed her under immense stress.

One morning, she was mating with Balaram in the bushes near the Kuhipat-Sasa Line road. Just then, a few tourist vehicles arrived. Maya moved onto the road and sat down. While the tourists busily clicked her pictures, she called out to Balaram who soon appeared on the road. To the astonishment of the visitors, they proceeded to mate right in front of the tourists.

The mating pair—Maya and Balaram

Maya walking on the Kuhipat road with her little cub

In September 2022, Maya gave birth for the fifth time. During this period, she wasn't seen by anyone for an entire month.

Then, on 1 October, she emerged onto the road with a tiny cub in her mouth, revealing she had given birth to just one cub this time. Coincidentally, Assistant Conservator of Forests (ACF) Mahesh Khore was passing along the Kuhipat road at the same time. Maya walked right in front of his vehicle, cub in mouth, allowing him to capture an exceptional photograph.

After that brief appearance, Maya wasn't seen again for the entire month. She stayed deep within the jungle to protect her newborn. However, true to her nature, by November, she began to make public appearances with the cub—a female—much to the delight of tourists.

Four months later, the same cub gave the forest staff quite a scare. The administration of the Tadoba reserve works tirelessly on various fronts to conserve the forest and wildlife. Along with regular patrolling, eco-tourism, engaging with locals and providing employment opportunities, one of their constant challenges is maintaining the natural habitat of the wildlife. For herbivores to thrive, the forest must offer suitable vegetation and food abundantly. Herbivores, in turn, sustain the population of carnivores. Invasive weeds and non-palatable plants (plants that animals avoid eating) often encroach on grazing grounds, so the forest department regularly uproots and replaces them with palatable flora.

That day, a team led by Forest Guard Niranjan Jude was marking boundaries for weed removal. The group included ten members, all walking along the Waghzari Nallah when they suddenly spotted Maya sitting ahead with her cub, now about four months old. They were just 50 feet away.

Recognizing the risk, Jude and his colleagues halted on the spot. Maya had noticed them, but she didn't react. However, the cub's curiosity was piqued, and it started trotting towards them. Jude quickly instructed everyone to huddle together, raise their sticks and back away cautiously. If Maya had followed the cub, the situation could have taken a serious turn. Fortunately, Maya remained put. After advancing 8 to 10 feet, the cub lost interest and turned back. The team managed to retreat safely.

Later, actual weed-clearing began near the Tadoba Lake area in Compartment 83. A group of female labourers were engaged in the task when one of them suddenly screamed, 'A tiger is coming!' Jude looked in the direction she pointed and saw Maya approaching from the Kala Amba side. He immediately instructed the labourers to get into the vehicle. By the time they climbed in, Maya had already come very close. Jude and a few others were still outside. Maya stopped just 40 to 45 feet away. She was calm, showing no signs of aggression. She stood there for a while, watching in silence. Then, she walked to the lake and settled in the water. Judging it best not to take any chances, Jude decided to leave the task for the day and quickly moved everyone to another compartment to continue the work.

Just eight days later, a similar incident unfolded in Compartment 90.

A Mother's Heart

Maya had to take extra precautions to keep her cub safe. She would hide the cub in a secure location before patrolling her territory to check for any male tigers other than Balaram nearby. At times, she climbed to high vantage points to assess potential threats. Only when she was sure of no danger would she bring the cub out of hiding.

In February 2023, Maya hunted a sambar near the Jamunbodi–Hilltop road. She was feasting on her meal just 50 metres off the road, with the cub by her side. Suddenly Rudra appeared on the scene, possibly drawn by the scent of the kill. His arrival posed a grave threat as he would undoubtedly kill the cub if he reached it. Sensing the danger, Maya quickly signalled it to flee. The frightened cub dashed away and reached the road where it froze in fear. It was hardly four months old and was visibly shaken. Confused and unsure of where to go, it anxiously waited for its mother.

Back in the bushes, Maya directly launched an attack on Rudra. Their roars shook the forest. Rudra, much stronger, not only deflected Maya's attack but also countered aggressively. The clash lasted mere seconds, long enough for Maya to realize she was clearly outmatched. However, she hadn't fought to win. With the cub safely out of reach, she reluctantly surrendered the kill to Rudra and retreated.

When Maya returned to the road, fresh wounds were visible on her front legs, but she paid no attention to them. Instead of approaching the road from the same spot where her cub had emerged, she cautiously came out from a different location. The cub saw its mother and ran to her. However, unlike her usual self, Maya didn't stop to lick or comfort it. Her only concern

Maya with her cub in tow, whom she fiercely protected from Rudra

was to leave the area as quickly as possible. She hurriedly started walking away, her body language a mix of urgency, fear and helplessness. The midday sun blazed overhead, and Maya was moving swiftly. The cub had to scramble to keep up. After a while, both mother and cub were visibly exhausted, foam forming at their mouths. But Maya couldn't afford to stop. She knew the danger hadn't passed yet.

She kept glancing back frequently, checking to ensure Rudra wasn't following. On the way, near Magar Tank, they came across a small puddle. Maya paused briefly, letting the tired cub drink water. She herself focused on keeping watch. The moment the cub finished, they resumed their flight. Just then, a sambar let out an alarm call! Maya froze. Had Rudra caught up with them? Her body stiffened, her face grim. She scanned the bushes on either side with her sharp eyes. It seemed she was preparing to face whatever was coming. But no tiger appeared. The sambar had possibly given the alarm call after spotting Maya herself.

She moved on quickly with the cub, eventually reaching the guest house near Tadoba Lake. From there, the pair slipped into the non-tourism zone behind the building, heading deeper toward the lake's sanctuary. Maya had used all her strength and strategy against Rudra that day. But how long could she keep this up?

The Tiger Anthem

MAYA'S FEMALE CUB WAS AS BOLD AND MISCHIEVOUS AS HER MOTHER. Together, the duo once again created a buzz, with their photos going viral on social media. On one occasion, Maya and her daughter were playfully splashing in the waters of the Tadoba Lake. Naturalist Himanshu Bagde's vehicle was the only one present at that time. Later he shared a video he had recorded on Instagram, where it garnered over 20 million views.

On 24 May 2023, *The Times of India* released a Hindi music video titled 'Tiger Anthem' on their social media platform. Featuring Maya and her cub, the anthem became a sensation across the country, amassing over 100 million views within the first fifteen days. The playful, poignant song, which celebrates the innocence of a cub growing up under its mother's care was penned by poet Tanveer Ghazi and set to a spirited tune by National Award-winning composer Shantanu Moitra. It was produced by internationally acclaimed filmmaker Subbiah Nalla Muthu.

Much of the anthem's appeal lay in Nalla Muthu's cinematography. His ability to frame the gentle, unguarded interactions between Maya and her cub—the cub darting between her legs, tugging at her playfully, embracing her neck—added an emotional depth that resonated widely. In one moment, Maya appears to momentarily shed her usual reserve, running and playing alongside her cub with childlike abandon.

A line from the song, 'Yeh pahaadiyaan, hari jhaadiyaan, yeh toh yunhi rahegi na, maa? (These hills and green bushes—will they always be here, mother?)', left a lasting impression. It was one of the first times a musical format had been used to convey a conservation message, and it struck a meaningful, lasting note.

Maya gently carrying her cub in front of tourists

Maya and her cub in a playful moment

Nalla Muthu, who had already produced six films for international channels, had carlicr gained widespread recognition for his film on Machli, the queen of Ranthambore. For the past four years, he had been shooting in Tadoba, documenting Maya's life. After hundreds of safaris and more than 400 hours of recorded footage, 'Tiger Anthem' was created using the material he had gathered.

The birth of this cub brought a renewed sense of vitality to Maya's life. Yet, beneath the surface, the challenges remained. Apart from Balaram, four other male tigers now roamed within Maya's territory, posing a continuous threat to the cub. But there was an additional challenge this time. Typically, tigresses have between two to five cubs, who play together and support each other when the mother is out hunting. Since this cub was entirely dependent on Maya's presence, she had to adjust her lifestyle. Maya, already ageing, had to spend extended periods with her cub, even playing with it occasionally.

Speaking about this phase in Maya's life, Nalla Muthu recalled to me, 'During this time, I developed a unique bond with Maya—a bond of trust. This was a testing period for her. She had to leave her four-month-old cub alone for hours. Before leaving, she would check from different spots if she could still spot the cub. Only after thoroughly inspecting the surroundings and ensuring the cub's safety would she leave. Sometimes, she would return after two or three hours, silently checking if the cub was safe, then leave again without making her presence known. Eventually, it got to the point where Maya would check from afar if our vehicle was there, and if it was, she would leave confidently. She believed that if we were present, her cub was safe. I never imagined that a tigress could trust humans to this extent. That was one of the happiest times of my life.'

But the moment passed all too quickly.

In March 2023, the cub was killed by a male tiger. Maya had once again suffered the devastating loss of a young one. Just days earlier, the cub had been seen walking with Balaram—thought to be its father—yet, even he could not prevent the tragedy.

The incident affected many who had followed Maya's story, including Nalla Muthu, who had developed a quiet emotional attachment to her and the cub. He paused filming and returned to Mumbai.

It was around this time that *The Times of India* approached him with the idea that would become 'Tiger Anthem'.

Maya vs Roma

By late 2022, noticeable changes had begun to appear in Maya. The colour of her right eye had altered, likely due to an infection or developing cataract. Such conditions in wild animals often resolve naturally, and at the time it wasn't considered a major concern. More concerning, however, was a partially broken canine, possibly the result of gnawing on a tough bone or a fight with another tiger. Losing a canine is a serious handicap for any tiger as it can hinder their hunting ability.

Yet Maya's spirit remained intact. She had overcome numerous challenges over the years. For over a decade, she had ruled the vast territories of Pandharpauni and its surrounding regions. No tiger had ever managed to defeat her or claim her territory. One incident, in particular, reaffirmed just how fiercely Maya defended her domain.

7 May 2023: In the dry heat of summer, wildlife sightings at waterholes are common, as most natural water sources dry up. But that year, unseasonal rains had left pools of water throughout the forest, lowering the likelihood of animals congregating at familiar spots. Vehicles of eager tourists were on the lookout for Maya. In the first two hours, only two or three vehicles caught a glimpse of her near the Magar Tank, which left the other tourists disappointed. They wandered across various roads within her territory, hoping for a sighting.

Eventually, some tourists reached Chital road and spotted a tigress near a waterhole. But upon closer inspection, the guides realized it wasn't Maya—it was Roma, Choti Tara's daughter. Choti Tara, nearly as old as Maya, ruled over Jamni Meadows. She had given birth to two female cubs three years ago: Bijli and Roma. Roma now had two cubs of her own and occupied a

The unsuspecting Roma as Maya launches a sudden attack

territory bordering Maya's. She hadn't been seen in over a month and now, here she was, inside Maya's territory.

After a while, Roma rose from the water and headed towards Jamunbodi. The tourist vehicles followed her at a safe distance. As she walked along the road, Roma left her scent on the trunk

Locked in a fierce clash,
Maya and Roma grapple for dominance

The younger, stronger Roma unable to withstand Maya's might

of a ghost tree before continuing her stroll. But she was unaware that she wasn't alone. Someone was stealthily trailing her.

No one knew when or how Maya had spotted Roma. The scene now resembled two golden rat snakes gliding along the red dirt road—Roma strolling casually ahead, and Maya following at a measured distance. Her face was tense and her movements cautious, but her gaze remained fixed on Roma. She was oblivious to the surrounding environment and the presence of tourist vehicles. Her sole focus was to teach this intruding tigress a lesson. Maya slightly lowered her head and trailed Roma closely. When Roma paused near a tree to mark her territory, Maya crouched down, pressing her belly to the ground, never taking her eyes off Roma. When Roma resumed walking, Maya did the same but quickened her pace. She was clearly about to launch a surprise attack. Roma sensed the danger and quickened her pace, trying to avoid a confrontation. But there was no way Maya would let her off easily.

Now in a crouch, she started running. The distance between them rapidly closed. With two great leaps, she reached Roma and confronted her head-on. Maya growled menacingly and Roma tried to respond with a defiant growl. The next moment, they attacked each other, their roars shaking the forest. Would Maya's decade-long reign crumble?

Within mere seconds of the initial skirmish, Roma surrendered. She lay flat on the ground, signalling her defeat. But Maya's rage wasn't yet quelled. Her body language showed her fierce anger. She began circling the seated Roma as if warning her. Whenever Roma tried to get up, Maya would charge at her, forcing her to sit back down. Then Maya would circle her again. This happened thrice. Finally, Roma seized an opportunity and bolted. Maya didn't chase her this time. She had already asserted her dominance.

When this encounter took place, Maya was over twelve years old, and Roma was just three.

Missing

In May 2023, while I was at Tadoba, Maya's territory was home to two male tigers—Balram and Mowgli. By mid-May, Maya had begun mating with both, and we expected her to give birth to her sixth litter around the first week of September.

Due to the monsoon, Maya's territory, along with the core area, was closed at the start of July. Despite the seasonal closure, forest department patrols continued as usual, and Maya was occasionally sighted. On 23 August, the caretaker at the forest rest house at Tadoba Lake spotted her near Panchdhara. By then, her belly was noticeably swollen.

As soon as tourism resumed on 1 October, visitors immediately began asking each other if anyone had seen Maya. Unfortunately, no one had. Within a week, *The Times of India* ran a story titled, 'Where Has Tadoba Queen Maya Gone?' The article raised concerns—had the reserve's most popular tigress vanished, or had she retreated into hiding after giving birth, keeping her distance from the busy tourist season?

Other newspapers and TV channels picked up the story, deepening the mystery of Maya's absence. The forest department officials and staff were not immediately alarmed. It was typical of Maya to remain hidden for a month or two after giving birth, only to reappear later, proudly presenting her cubs. They believed this could be another such instance. Still, with no sightings even into the first week of October and growing anxiety among her fans, the forest department decided to act. Camera traps were set up across the Tadoba and Kolara ranges—Maya's known territories. The ranges were divided into grids, each covering 2 square kilometres. A total of 145 grids were created, each fitted with one camera trap. The operation began

Advancing age, one eye showing signs of change and a broken canine

on 7 October, and by that evening itself, the analysis of captured images commenced. The results revealed the presence of seven female and nine male adult tigers in the Tadoba and Kolara zones, along with four cubs. But there was still no sign of Maya. What was even more striking was the presence of three tigresses—Choti Tara, Bijli and Roma—within Maya's territory. Maya had never allowed any other tigress into her territory, but now Choti Tara, nearly the same age as Maya, and her two daughters were moving around confidently.

This led to one conclusion—Maya was no longer in her territory. But where was she?

The forest department expanded its search, initiating camera trapping in the Palasgaon range towards Shivani and Khadsangi range towards Chimur areas as well. Large-scale patrolling was also underway with the help of forest guards and labourers. But the search was far from easy. That year, the monsoon had lingered, leaving low-lying areas in the forest waterlogged.

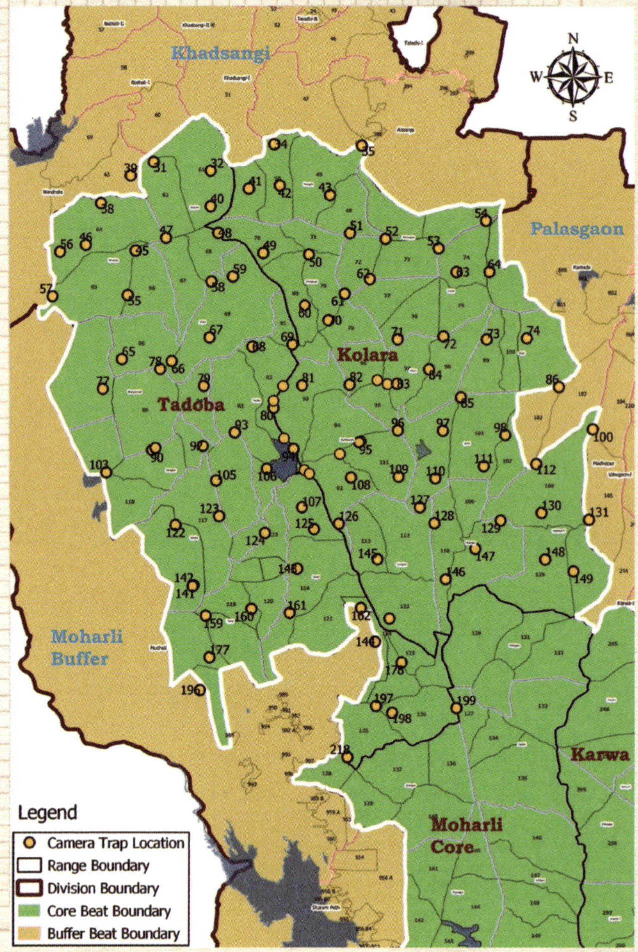

Map showing the forest department's camera trapping grid across Tadoba and Kolara ranges during the search for Maya

Dense vegetation and tall grass had grown everywhere, making some parts of the jungle completely inaccessible. Despite these obstacles, the staff continued their patrols with utmost caution. Like the tourists and photographers, she was also dearly loved by the forest department staff. Everyone was concerned for her safety. Everyone hoped she would be found safe.

Search Operation

Despite relentless efforts through camera trapping and patrolling, Maya's whereabouts remained unknown. Pressure on the forest department from her admirers continued to escalate. Social media and news outlets buzzed with constant speculation, with her well-wishers praying for her safety. As a last resort, the department devised a plan to launch a special search operation in her territory from 16 to 18 November. The mission involved thorough foot patrols to meticulously comb every nook and corner of the area.

The special operation commenced on the morning of 16 November. A total of 150 individuals, including forest officers, guards, labourers and STPF personnel, participated in the mission. Five teams were formed to cover the territory, walk through the jungle and examine each section of the terrain.

The first two days yielded no significant findings. On the third, while searching Tadoba Beat in Tadoba range, one team spotted something lying in the grass in Compartment 82. As they drew closer, their hearts sank—it was a skeleton. At first glance, it appeared to be the remains of a tiger. Senior officers, along with veterinary officer Dr Ravikant Khobragade, rushed to the site. The bones were scattered within a hundred-meter radius. They were collected carefully, but as the skin, flesh and organs had already decomposed, no necropsy could be performed. Samples of the bones were sent to the National Centre for Biological Sciences (NCBS) in Bangalore for DNA analysis. Fortunately, Maya's DNA samples had earlier been collected for a scientific study, enabling a comparison.

News of the discovery spread like wildfire. Newspapers ran headlines such as 'Is Maya Tigress Dead?' and 'Death of Tigress

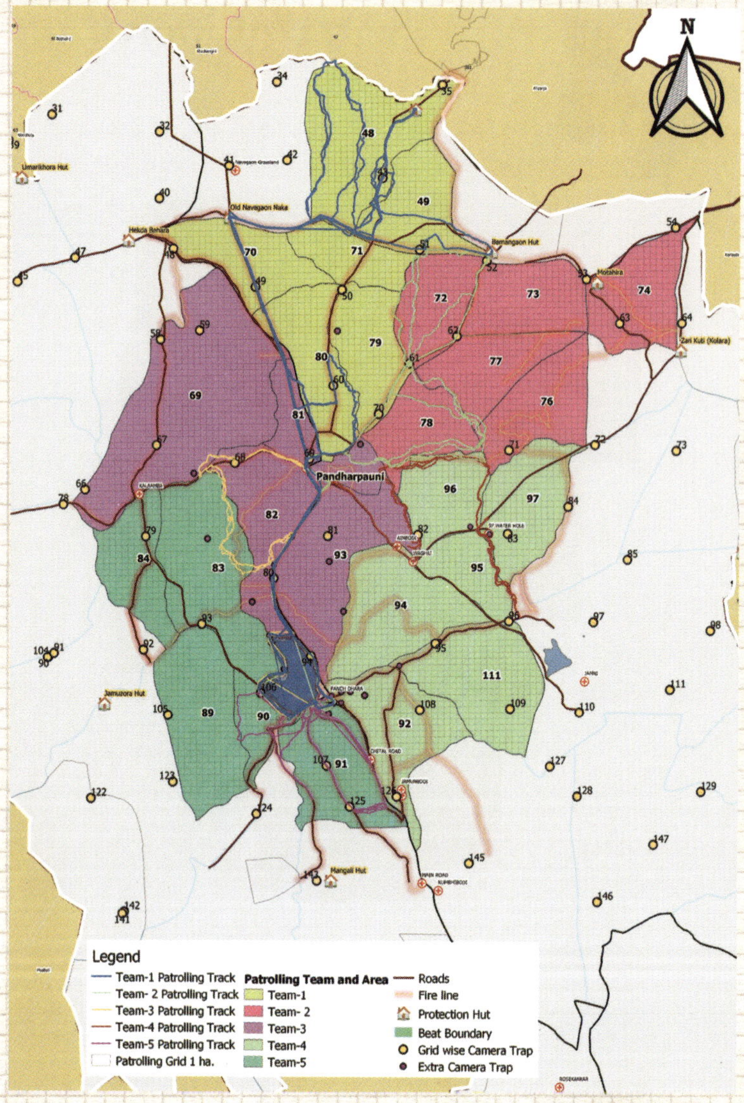

Details of the patrol routes undertaken by the forest department to trace Maya's whereabouts

Maya?' on their front pages. Her fans were plunged into sorrow. Calls started pouring in as people sought confirmation of the news. WhatsApp messages circulated rapidly, and social media was flooded with tributes to Maya. Thousands of photos and videos of Maya were shared, as people recalled their memories of her over the past thirteen years. Some even printed posters in her memory. Meanwhile, the phones in the offices of the field director, core and buffer deputy directors kept ringing non-stop. Everyone sought updates and confirmation.

Finally, on 21 November, the Tadoba administration issued an official press release. It stated that the forest department had not officially declared Maya's death. The species, age and gender of the remains found during the search operation could only be determined after receiving the DNA analysis report. The note urged people not to spread rumours or draw premature conclusions.

Maya's fans clung to hope. Occasionally, reports of her sighting would surface, but they all turned out to be false. On 3 January 2024, a Hindi-language newspaper ran a headline, 'Aakhirkar Mil Gayi Maya' ('Finally, Maya Found'). Along with the news, they printed an old photograph of Maya peeking from behind a milestone marked 'Tadoba 1 kilometre'. The report, unsurprisingly, was inaccurate.

Then came the report from the NCBS Bangalore. It revealed that the bones did not belong to a tiger, but to a herbivore. Once again, hope bloomed among her fans.

It's All Maya!

Days turned into weeks. The forest department continued its camera trapping and regular patrolling. Maya was nowhere to be found. Tigresses like Choti Tara, Bijli and Roma had taken over and settled into her former territory. But Maya did not return to reclaim her kingdom. Why did this happen? What might have happened? Where could she have gone?

No one has definitive answers to these questions, but a few theories exist.

When Maya went missing, she was pregnant. As always, she faced threats from male tigers. To ensure a safe delivery, she might have left her territory in search of a secure location—and simply never returned.

Camera traps had revealed an uptick in young tigresses in Maya's territory. One of them could have driven Maya out.

Another possibility is that she could have been involved in a confrontation with a rival tigress or an intruding male tiger. She might have sustained a fatal injury and succumbed to them.

Tigers in the wild live, on average, ten to fifteen years. Maya was nearly thirteen. She may have died of natural causes. It's estimated that only about 20 per cent of wild tigers who die naturally are ever found. So even if she did die of natural causes, her remains may never be recovered.

Whichever version of events you believe, one fact is hard to escape: Maya is unlikely to return. Even if, against all odds, she's still alive, her time as the Queen of Tadoba has ended. Pandharpauni no longer belongs to her. Maya's story often felt larger than life. It seems only fitting then that her disappearance should remain unresolved—leaving us caught between hope and acceptance.

The dramatic tale of Maya concluded mysteriously

Maya's sudden disappearance left her fans suspended between hope and acceptance

Afterword

I grew up completely unaware of jungles and wildlife. In 2008, I visited Tadoba for the first time with my wife. We didn't see any tigers—not then, not for the first four years—but we both fell in love with the place. The forest, the animals, and the birds captivated us in ways we hadn't expected.

I first encountered Maya in 2018. She passed so close to our Gypsy that I could have touched her had I extended my hand. I was inside, filming on my phone—this was before mobile phones were banned in Tadoba, a decision I now fully support. As she walked by, Maya stopped and locked eyes with me. For a moment, it felt like a jolt of lightning struck my heart in that instant. That moment still replays in slow motion in my mind. After that, I saw her frequently, and my affection for her only deepened.

In 2021, when I started working directly with the Tadoba administration, my love for wildlife and my understanding of conservation took on a new dimension. I realized that while each tiger is important, conservation is about the survival of the entire species. I learned to view tigers not just through emotion, but also with the objectivity of a researcher. That shift in perspective helped me write about Maya with both care and clarity, relying on facts and evidence.

Some of my colleagues argue that Maya's contribution to tiger conservation in and around Tadoba was limited. She successfully raised only two cubs, both male. In comparison, tigresses like Madhuri, Choti Tara and Sonam played a more significant role in increasing the tiger population. It is true Maya did not pass on her territory to her offspring. However, it is equally true that none of the other tigresses had to face the kind of challenges Maya did. Unfortunately for Maya, male tigers searching for territories consistently targeted hers, at times five of them simultaneously. Defending her cubs from the powerful males while holding onto her territory was a delicate balancing act. One that she managed for years.

Some claim that Maya was a careless mother, indifferent to her cubs. They say she would often leave them unattended, and this neglect got them killed. I see little merit in this argument. Life in the wild for a tiger is tough at the best of times; for a tigress raising cubs, it's even harder. Maya had to hunt to feed herself and young, mark her territory to protect it and keep rival males away—all while nurturing her cubs. Sometimes she succeeded, sometimes she failed.

It is suggested that Maya could have avoided the relentless pressure from the male tigers by giving up her territory to protect her cubs better. Many tigresses had done so by leaving their territories and, in doing so, saved both themselves and their cubs. But Maya was different. Her territory wasn't just a stretch of land—it was the most resource-rich expanse in Tadoba, abundant in water and prey. She fiercely defended it for 11 years even though her mother and grandmother hadn't managed to hold on to it. That she chose to defend her precious empire is hardly surprising.

Another view holds that Maya's fame was a result of her living in the tourist zone, questioning her celebrity. While it is true that she was frequently seen by tourists, her popularity stemmed from more than visibility. Just as two siblings can have entirely different temperaments, Maya's nature was different from other tigresses. Her ease around tourists made her a favourite—and in time a global icon.

Still others point to the human lives she took. However, in each unfortunate incident, the person was either sitting or crouching when attacked —positions that to a tiger mimic prey. Maya acted according to instinct. The claim that she developed a taste for human blood does not stand to scrutiny. Had that been the case, it would have been impossible for forest staff to work in her territory, and tourism would have been shut down. On the contrary, there are numerous instances where Maya came face-to-face with forest staff on patrol or working in the area and did not cause any harm whatsoever.

It's true that Maya did not help significantly increase the tiger population. But her contribution to Tadoba's visibility—and by extension, to conservation—is undeniable. Her frequent sightings, her confidence, her playful cubs, her hunting prowess, and the mythology surrounding her kept drawing tourists in droves. The revenue generated from increased tourism provided funds that the forest department could use for conservation efforts. Moreover, it created employment for thousands of locals, fostering greater community involvement in conservation.

But Maya's most enduring contribution lies elsewhere. She sparked a love for tigers in millions of people. I've met many individuals who were mildly curious about tigers but didn't feel any emotional connection. After seeing Maya, they fell in love with tigers. They returned to Tadoba again and again. They explored other tiger reserves. They learned more about tigers. This ripple of unintended, yet transformative public awareness is Maya's greatest legacy.

Of course, tiger conservation is a long-term, ongoing process. While each tiger is important, the conservation effort cannot revolve around just one. Maya's absence will not stop this cycle. Today, Choti Tara has taken her place; tomorrow, it will be another tigress. This cycle will continue.

And yet, for all of us who witnessed this story unfold, for those who saw her in her glory—there will always be a special place in our hearts for the true queen of Tadoba: Maya.

At the bank of
the watering hole

Maya's Lineage

Mohacha Khadda Female

Bandi

Leela + Hilltop Male

P1 T12 P3 Pandu

Maya (T12) + Gabbar (T37)

Cub1 Cub2

Maya (T12) + Namdev (T42)

Cub1 Cub2 Cub3

Maya (T12) + Matkasur (T49)

Surya Meera

Maya (T12) + Tala (T100)

Cub1 Cub2 Cub3 Cub4 Y Mark (T201) Maya (T12) + Balram (T168)

Cub1

Maya's regal walk will always be remembered

Life Cycle of a Tiger

The life cycle of a tiger in its natural habitat, i.e., the forest, typically unfolds through the following stages:

Mating between a male and female tiger lasts for about a week

↓

After a gestation period of 102 to 108 days, the tigress gives birth to a litter of two to five cubs

↓

The cubs' eyes open within six to twelve days of birth

↓

For the first two to three months, the cubs rely entirely on their mother's milk

↓

Around the one-year mark, they begin accompanying their mother on hunting trips

↓

Between eighteen and twenty-eight months of age, the cubs separate from their mother and begin life independently

↓

Tigers reach sexual maturity between three and five years of age

↓

In the wild, a tiger's average lifespan ranges from ten to fifteen years

Statues of Maya and her cubs at the Moharli gate

Author's Note & Acknowledgements

In 2023, while editing *Enchanting Tadoba*, a coffee-table book for the Tadoba-Andhari Tiger Reserve (TATR), a compelling idea took root in me: why not create a book devoted entirely to Maya?

The more I explored her story, it felt less like the life of a tigress and more like that of a cinematic heroine. There was everything—emotion, drama, striking visuals and unforgettable moments. To capture that richness through photographs alone felt inadequate. Maya's journey deserved a narrative of its own.

I shared this idea with Dr Jitendra Ramgaokar, the then field director of Tadoba-Andhari Tiger Reserve, who offered his support immediately. Encouraged, I began work on what would eventually become *Ek Hoti Maya* in Marathi. As a longtime admirer of Maya, I soon discovered many others who felt the same way. Some shared personal encounters, others contributed striking photographs that now appear in this volume. Forest officials, staff and even daily-wage forest workers generously recounted their memories, helping bring Maya's story to life with depth and texture.

Yet, I did not want this book to be a patchwork of anecdotes. I wanted the writing to rest on solid ground. So I consulted various forest department records and cross-checked events and observations with experienced wildlife experts and enthusiasts. Where accounts diverged, I chose the most plausible and well-supported versions. Any remaining errors are entirely my own.

As a tigress from Tadoba's tourism zone, Maya was constantly in the spotlight. She received more love and attention from tourists than any other tiger in the area. Losing her mother early, she inherited a prime territory rich in water and prey, which she defended fiercely. Her distinctive, unusually friendly and relaxed encounters with tourists earned her the title of the most photographed tigress in Tadoba. However, many might not know that this same tigress had also claimed the lives of four humans in the forest. Her story, like all lives lived in the wild, was layered.

Maya was one of the most recognized and admired tigresses in Tadoba. A skilled hunter, sharp strategist, and fierce defender of her territory, she was also a favourite among photographers and tourists. But her life was far from easy. With multiple males frequently encroaching on her range, she had to fight on many fronts, and as a result, managed to raise only a few of her cubs. It was this constant tension—the balance between strength and vulnerability—that drew me deeper into her story and inspired this book.

The primary goal of this book was to provide readers an intimate glimpse into the arduous life of a tiger, told through Maya's journey. I hope this narrative inspires empathy, respect and a deeper appreciation for the life of wild tigers. The Marathi edition succeeded at doing that. Published in 2024, it received an overwhelming response and won the Lokmat Sahitya Puraskar and Aranyarishi Maruti Chitampalli Award by Vidarbh Sahitya Sangh. The growing interest in Maya's story encouraged me to revisit and expand it for this English edition.

My special thanks to former Field Director Dr Jitendra Ramgaokar and former deputy director (core) Nandkishore Kale for their steady guidance. Wildlife biologist Prajakta Hushangabadkar, Maya's ardent fan Himanshu Bagde and Tadoba's own living encyclopaedia, Roshan Katkar, supported me like family. Forest guard Sheetal Kulmethe generously shared notes from her personal diary. My wife, Surekha Sonawane, my first reader, provided invaluable suggestions. My mother, Vasanti Sonawane, gave me blessings and encouragement, and my dearest friend Vanita Kamble and other friends the emotional strength needed to finish the book. The support of senior officials, frontline staff, safari guides, wildlife photographers and tourists was invaluable. Without them, this book would not have taken shape.

I am very thankful to the present field director of the reserve, Dr Prabhu Nath Shukla, for his cooperation. Last but not least, a very special thanks to Shiv Sena chief Uddhav Thackeray for his encouragement, and to legendary cricketer Sachin Tendulkar for writing the foreword to this book.

Much has changed since the inception of this book idea. Maya has now disappeared—an end as dramatic as the life she led. In her absence, Choti Tara and her daughters now rule her kingdom. But Tadoba echoes with memories of Maya. Even today, visitors find themselves scanning the Pandharpauni waterholes, hoping for one last glimpse of the queen.

No one knows whether Maya is alive. But for those who followed her story—and for me—she will always remain in our hearts.

ANANT SONAWANE
29 July 2025

Special Thanks To

Tadoba-Andhari Tiger Reserve (TATR)

Dr Jitendra Ramgaokar, Indian Forest Service (IFS), Chief Conservator of Forests (CCF) and former Field Director
Dr Prabhu Nath Shukla, IFS, Conservator of Forests (CF) and Field Director
Nandkishore Kale, IFS, former Deputy Director (Core)
Anand Reddy, IFS, Deputy Director (Core)
Kushagra Pathak, IFS, Deputy Director (Buffer)
Piyusha Jagtap, IFS, former Deputy Director (Buffer)
Mahesh Khore, former Assistant Conservator of Forests (Core)
Saitanmay Dubey, Assistant Conservator of Forests (Buffer)
Shatanik Bhagwat, former Divisional Forest Officer
Sachin Shinde, Divisional Forest Officer
Satish Shende, former Range Forest Officer, Tadoba Range
Bhavik Chivande, Range Forest Officer, Tadoba Range
Pradeep Chavan, former Range Forest Officer, Kolara Range
Arunkumar Gond, Range Forest Officer, Moharli Range
Manisha Jadhav, former Range Forest Officer, Special Tiger Protection Force (STPF), Chimur
Sheetal Kulmethe, former Forest Guard, Tadoba Range
Niranjan Jude, Forest Guard, Tadoba Range
Rama Warbhe, former Forest Labourer
Dr Ravikant Khobragade, Veterinary Officer (Wildlife)
Prajakta Hushangabadkar, former Wildlife Biologist
Yashaswi Rao, former Wildlife Biologist
Shahebaj Sheikh, Geographic Information Systems (GIS) Specialist

Prafulla Savarkar, Environmental Education Officer
Saket Agasti, Sociologist
Akhil Rainchwar, Clerk, TATR Conservation Foundation

All safari guides and staff of the reserve;
my best friends—Vanita Kamble, Sachin Bhanap, Mahendra Mandlik, Sandeep Bidaye and Rajeev Anikhindi.

Image Credits

1. The queen of Tadoba. Photo courtesy Harshal Malvankar
2. The 2023 tourism season began without any sighting of her. Photo courtesy Shivani Deshpande
3. Inked paw print of the tigress Leela. Photo courtesy TATR
4. The courting pair—Leela and Hilltop Male. Photo courtesy Sandeep Gujar
5. P2 with her mother, Leela. Photo courtesy Varun Thakkar
6. The ever-curious P2, always seeking something new. Photo courtesy Himanshu Bagde
7. Curious, bold and aggressive P2 with her mother. Photo courtesy Himanshu Bagde
8. P2 inspecting the forest guard's motorcycle. Photo courtesy Himanshu Bagde
9. Waiting for the right moment. Photo courtesy Himanshu Bagde
10. A sudden strike on the prey. Photo courtesy Himanshu Bagde
11. Mounted on the boar's back. Photo courtesy Himanshu Bagde
12. Maya had the upper hand from the very first move. Photo courtesy Himanshu Bagde
13. Determination versus brute strength. Photo courtesy Himanshu Bagde
14. Her first major hunt. Photo courtesy Himanshu Bagde
15. The last time the family was seen together. Photo courtesy Farooque Khan
16. Bearing the weight of her new territory and the loss of her mother. Photo courtesy Deep Kathikar
17. Distraught after her mother's death. Photo courtesy Sandeep Gujar
18. Maya learning about how to become a hunter. Photo

courtesy Swethakumar Rangarao Bobbili

19. A map of Maya's territory. Photo courtesy TATR
20. Maya marking her territory. Photo courtesy Mahesh Khore
21. Maya tenderly caring for a spotted deer fawn, as if it were her own cub. Photo courtesy Ravin Jadhav
22. An illustration depicting Maya's attack. Illustration courtesy Shreya Khadilkar
23. Gabbar, Maya's first partner. Photo courtesy Varun Thakkar
24. A queen in her element—Maya, with the aura of a screen legend. Photo courtesy Sadaa Sayed
25. The first-time mother, carefully relocating one of her cubs to a safer place. Photo courtesy Yogesh Paradkar
26. Grief in motion: Maya wanders the forest, looking for her lost cubs. Photo courtesy Himanshu Bagde
27. The 'M' on her shoulder made her 'Maya' to the world, but to the forest staff she was T12. Photo courtesy Mahesh Khore
28. Maya and the villagers: a rare coexistence. Photo courtesy Mahesh Khore
29. The beloved tigress of the forest workers. Photo courtesy Rundan Katkar
30. At 97 waterhole, Maya mates with Gabbar. Photo courtesy Himanshu Bagde
31. Maya's cubs frolicking at Pandharpauni. Photo courtesy Aishwarya Sridhar
32. Maya and her three cubs. Photo courtesy Jaya Rane
33. Maya with her cub in an embrace. Photo courtesy Ricky Patel
34. Maya and her cub, immortalized on a postage stamp. Public domain
35. Learning to kill: Maya's cubs launch an attack on a gaur. Photo courtesy Aishwarya Sridhar
36. Moment of reckoning: Maya's cubs make their first

independent kill—a barking deer. Photo courtesy Aishwarya Sridhar

37. The wild dog pair, lost in their courtship. Photo courtesy Sudeep Mehta
38. Maya, waiting for the right moment. Photo courtesy Sudeep Mehta
39. The ambush—Maya launches her sudden attack. Photo courtesy Sudeep Mehta
40. One swift, lethal strike ends the chase. Photo courtesy Sudeep Mehta
41. A successful hunt. Photo courtesy Sudeep Mehta
42. A visual interpretation of the fatal incident involving Maya. Illustration courtesy Shreya Khadilkar
43. Matkasur, who may have played a role in Mangaldas's death. Photo courtesy Himanshu Bagde
44. Bhola, the lone surviving cub, halts traffic on the Pandharpauni–Navegaon road. Photo courtesy Himanshu Bagde
45. Maya's fierce clash with Matkasur at Pandharpauni-2. Photos courtesy Jaya Rane
46. Maya with her trophy after a successful, calculated strike. Photo courtesy Himanshu Bagde
47. Maya's anger—a rare glimpse for tourists. Photo courtesy Aishwarya Sridhar
48. Maya's response was a reminder that she was a wild predator, not a spectacle. Photo courtesy Aishwarya Sridhar
49. Surya and Meera, sheltered under the watchful presence of Maya. Photo courtesy Himanshu Bagde
50. The siblings on the verge of being separated from their mother. Photo courtesy Manisha Jadhav
51. Maya in an aggressive stance as Chota Matka surrenders completely. Photos courtesy Manisha Jadhav
52. Surya with his mother. Photo courtesy Sumeet Khare

53. Surya and Meera attempting to surround the gaur. Photo courtesy Roshan Katkar
54. Meera bearing deep wounds in her final days. Photo courtesy Roshan Katkar
55. Maya retreating into seclusion after injuring her left eye. Photo courtesy Manisha Jadhav
56. Maya's behaviour could sometimes leave everyone puzzled. Photo courtesy Roshan Katkar
57. The mating pair—Tala and Maya. Photo courtesy Roshan Katkar
58. Rudra and Maya. Photo courtesy Vishal Bane
59. Maya hunting a sambar fawn. Photo courtesy Mohammad Salman
60. The newborn cubs nestled in a rocky crevice near the Waghai stream—Maya's fourth litter. Photo courtesy Sheetal Kulmethe
61. Maya with her four cubs at Pandharpauni. Photo courtesy Himanshu Bagde
62. Maya communicating with her cubs by just wagging her tail. Photo courtesy Aishwarya Sridhar
63. A mother fulfilling her responsibility by hunting for her family. Photo courtesy Akshay Ghag
64. An illustration of the alleged scene of the incident. Illustration courtesy Shreya Khadilkar
65. Maya's international screen debut in Tiger Queen of Taru (2021)
66. The queen in her capital, Pandharpauni. Photo courtesy Himanshu Bagde
67. A tiger hunts only when hungry. Photo courtesy Manisha Jadhav
68. Maya's adventurous cubs wished to hunt a gaur. Photo courtesy Himanshu Bagde
69. The STPF personnel often encountered Maya. Photo courtesy Nikhil Abhyankar

70. An imagined rendering of the incident scene. Photo courtesy Shreya Khadilkar
71. Maya, moments before the tragic encounter with Swati Dhumane's team. Photo courtesy Swastika Talukdar
72. A map depicting the events leading to the death of the forest guard's tragic death. Photo courtesy TATR
73. Although Maya was affectionate, she was still a wild tiger in her natural habitat. Photo courtesy Himanshu Bagde
74. Maya was friendly, but surviving a night on foot in her territory was nothing short of a miracle. Photo courtesy Himanshu Bagde
75. Maya's reactions were always hard to predict. Photo courtesy Neeraj Gade
76. The mating pair—Maya and Balaram. Photo courtesy Nikhil Abhyankar
77. Maya walking on the Kuhipat road with her little cub. Photo courtesy Mahesh Khore
78. Maya walking with her cub to protect it from Rudra. Photo courtesy Sadaa Sayed
79. Maya gently carrying her cub in front of tourists. Photo courtesy Gaurav Dhotre
80. Maya and her cub in a playful moment. Photo courtesy Sadaa Sayed
81. The unsuspecting Roma as Maya launches a sudden attack. Photo courtesy Sadaa Sayed
82. Locked in a fierce clash, Maya and Roma grapple for dominance. Photo courtesy Sadaa Sayed
83. The younger, stronger Roma unable to withstand Maya's might. Photo courtesy Sadaa Sayed
84. Advancing age, one eye showing signs of change and a broken canine. Photo courtesy Neeraj Gade
85. Map showing the forest department's camera trapping grid across Tadoba and Kolara ranges during the search for Maya. Photo courtesy TATR

86. Details of the patrol routes undertaken by the forest department to trace Maya's whereabouts. Photo courtesy TATR
87. The dramatic tale of Maya concluded mysteriously. Photo courtesy Mahesh Khore
88. Maya's sudden disappearance left her fans suspended between hope and acceptance. Photo courtesy Uddhav Thackeray
89. At the bank of the watering hole. Photo courtesy Saurabh Tamne
90. Maya's regal walk will always be remembered. Photo courtesy Ankita Malvankar
91. Maya and one of her cubs. Photo courtesy Uddhav Thackeray
92. Statue of Maya and her cubs at the Moharli Gate. Photo courtesy Roshan Katkar
93. Maya in motion. Photo courtesy Harshal Malvankar

About the Author

ANANT SONAWANE is a journalist turned conservation communicator and storyteller who works at the intersection of science, wildlife and public engagement. Since 2021, he has served as the communications officer for the Tadoba – Andhari Tiger Reserve and is the executive editor of *Tadoba Diaries*, the reserve's monthly newsletter. With over two decades of experience in journalism, he has held leadership roles across print, television and financial news, including Aaj Dinank, Sakal, Tarun Bharat, Zee 24 Taas, ETV, Times Now and the news agency Cogencis (now Informist). A committed advocate for wildlife and environmental conservation, he founded *Ranvata*, the first Marathi web magazine dedicated to these issues. Sonawane is a founding member of the Indian Ecologic Foundation and the author of *Ek Hoti Maya*, winner of the Lokmat Sahitya Puraskar and the Aranya Rishi Maruti Chitampalli Puraskar.

HarperCollinsPublishersIndia

At HarperCollins India, we believe in telling the best stories and finding the widest readership for our books in every format possible. We started publishing in 1992; a great deal has changed since then, but what has remained constant is the passion with which our authors write their books, the love with which readers receive them, and the sheer joy and excitement that we as publishers feel in being a part of the publishing process.

Over the years, we've had the pleasure of publishing some of the finest writing from the subcontinent and around the world, including several award-winning titles and some of the biggest bestsellers in India's publishing history. But nothing has meant more to us than the fact that millions of people have read the books we published, and that somewhere, a book of ours might have made a difference.

As we look to the future, we go back to that one word—a word which has been a driving force for us all these years.

Read.

Harper Collins · Harper Sport · HARPER FICTION · HARPER NON-FICTION · हार्पर हिन्दी

HARPER LEARNING · HARPER VANTAGE · HCCB HARPERCOLLINS CHILDREN'S BOOKS · 4th · HARPER PERENNIAL

HARPER DESIGN · BOOKTOPUS · HARPER BUSINESS